S0-AQL-259

THE
BIBLE
ALONE?

IS THE BIBLE ALONE SUFFICIENT?

EDITED BY MARCUS GRODI

CHResources
Zanesville, Ohio

CHResources
PO Box 8290
Zanesville, OH 43702
740–450–1175
www.chnetwork.org

CHResources is a registered trademark
of the Coming Home Network International, Inc.

Cover design and page layout by Jennifer Bitler
www.doxologydesign.com

CONTENTS

INTRODUCTION:
THE SIGNIFICANCE OF PHILIP

Is the Bible *alone* truly sufficient for all matters of faith? This is what millions of Christians believe, or at least the presumption upon which they base most of what they believe. It's what I believed for most of my life, and what I assumed most Christians have always believed. But is it true?

It was a shock to me when I learned that this was not the usual view of Christians before Martin Luther made the following bold statement, in 1521, at the Diet of Worms:

> Unless I am convinced by the testimony of the Holy Scriptures or by evident reason — for I can believe neither pope nor councils alone, as it is clear that they have erred repeatedly and contradicted themselves — I consider myself convicted by the testimony of Holy Scripture, which is my basis; my conscience is captive to the Word of God. Thus I cannot and will not retract, because acting against one's conscience is neither safe nor sound. God help me. Amen.[1]

On the surface, this conviction sounds like a gallant and faithful declaration of the sufficiency of the divinely inspired Word of God. Yet, given the historical trajectory and subsequent effect of Luther's words, was this bold proclamation also a tacit approval of the other two foundations upon which Luther took his stand: "evident reason" and "conscience"? For nearly five hundred years, well-meaning Christians, using what they considered "evident reason" to form "conscience" based on "the testimony of Holy Scripture," have accepted, pro-

---

1   As quoted in Heiko A. Oberman, *Luther: Man Between God and the Devil*; trans. Eileen Walliser-Schwarzbart (New York: Image Books, 1989), p. 39; quoting *Reichstagsakten* 2.581, 23–582, 2.

moted, and defended all kinds of theological and moral opinions, which has led to thousands of divisions. Today, there are Bible-alone believers who no longer believe in the traditional doctrines of the Trinity, the divinity of Christ, the necessity of Baptism, or even the Church, and, influenced by culture, have come to accept, promote, and defend such "rights" as contraception, abortion, euthanasia, same-sex "marriage," as well as a long list of contemporary alternative lifestyles.

But does this necessarily mean that there's something wrong with relying on the Bible *alone*? A clue to this starts to emerge in the story of Philip and the Ethiopian eunuch.

Once upon a time, there was an Ethiopian eunuch, a court official of Candace, Queen of the Ethiopians. He was in charge of all her treasure. The eunuch had come to Jerusalem to worship, and the Apostle Philip had been led by an angel to go and meet him. As the Ethiopian official was on his way back home, Philip found him riding in his chariot and reading the prophet Isaiah.

Now, of course, I'm not making this story up. It's found in Acts 8:26–40. Few details are given about the background of this African eunuch; we don't know what specifically he believed and why he traveled all the way up to Jerusalem to worship. And where and how he got a personal copy of the Book of Isaiah. This of course had to be a hand-copied scroll — for the printing press was still nearly fourteen hundred years away — and therefore would have been expensive and rare. It is important to realize that in those days, people didn't have copies of the Old Testament Scriptures lying around on their coffee tables. That phenomenon did not evolve for many, many centuries.

When Philip encountered the official, he asked if the African understood what he was reading. The eunuch's response indicates that his difficulty was not an inability to read the language, which would either have been Hebrew or Greek (the latter, if the version he was reading was the Septuagint translation). No, the problem was one of *interpretation*, for he responded in verse 31, "How can I [understand], unless some one guides me?"

For those adhering to the doctrine of *sola Scriptura*, or the "Bible *alone*," this account should stand as a stumbling block. The apparently well-educated Ethiopian official was reading one of the clearest prophecies from Isaiah (cf. 53:7–8) about the Suffering Servant-Messiah:

> As a sheep led to the slaughter
> or a lamb before its shearer is silent,
> so he opens not his mouth.
> In his humiliation justice was denied him.
> Who can describe his generation?
> For his life is taken up from the earth.

The Ethiopian then asked Philip, "Please, about whom does the prophet say this, about himself or about some one else?"

Now let's pull ourselves away from the Ethiopian's specific question and Philip's response, and recognize the significance of what is happening: the written biblical prophecy *alone* was apparently not sufficient to lead this man to Christ, or to faith and therefore salvation. A human witness and interpreter was needed.

Some might respond that Philip's answer as well as those given later by Paul, Peter, James, John, Matthew, Luke, etc., became the New Testament, which thereby explained the meaning of this and other Old Testament prophecies for any who would ever need an answer. If this is true, then why are there still thousands upon thousands of sermons being preached, Bible commentaries being published, and Bible studies being led all over the world, if further explanation isn't necessary?

Is it because, just as this highly motivated Ethiopian eunuch recognized, one cannot understand the eternal significance of the Scriptures unless "someone guides"? One could argue, "The eunuch could not understand because he had not yet been given the Holy Spirit. Christians, however, have been given the Holy Spirit to provide this guidance! As it says in First John, 'you have been anointed by the Holy One, and you all know … you have no need that any one should teach you; as his anointing teaches you about everything'" (1 Jn 2:20, 27).

If so, then why so much confusion, contradiction, even conflict among Christians? If one were to argue that only those Christians who have been anointed with the Holy Spirit interpret Scripture correctly, this only raises the "chicken and the egg" question: Does having, what one considers, the correct interpretation prove the anointing of the Spirit, or does having, what one considers, the anointing of the Holy Spirit prove the correct interpretation?

And the very quote from First John disclaims this argument, because if what St. John wrote was literally true for the spirit-filled Christians to whom he was writing, why then did he need to write it? Shouldn't they have already known this through their anointing?

No, just as the encounter between the Apostle Philip and the eunuch so clearly reveals, Jesus sent forth His hand-chosen and anointed apostolic band to make disciples and teach the whole world (Mt 28:19–20) about who He was and about salvation.

It is our prayer that this short book will affirm the importance of Scripture as a divinely given foundation for our faith, but also encourage the reader to consider the need for the authority established by Christ for its trustworthy interpretation.

SOME PRACTICAL PROBLEMS WITH *SOLA SCRIPTURA*[2]

JIMMY AKIN

Simply stated, the Protestant doctrine of sola Scriptura ("Scripture alone") claims that every teaching in Christian theology (everything pertaining to "faith and practice") must be able to be derived from Scripture alone. This is expressed by the Reformation slogan Quod non est biblicum, non est theologicum *("What is not biblical is not theological").[3]*

An essential part of this doctrine, as historically articulated by Protestants, is that theology must be done without allowing Tradition or a Magisterium (teaching authority) any binding authority. If Tradition or a Magisterium could bind the conscience of the believer as to what he must believe then the believer would not be looking to Scripture alone as his authority.

A necessary corollary of the doctrine of *sola Scriptura* is, therefore, the idea of an absolute right of private judgment in the interpretation of the Scriptures. Each individual has the final prerogative to decide for himself what the correct interpretation of a given passage of Scripture means, irrespective of

---

2 This is a revised version of an article by Jimmy Akin originally titled "The Practical Problems of *Sola Scriptura*" that was previously published in the Coming Home Network International's *Sola Scriptura* journal. Reprinted with permission.

3 Cf. Richard A. Muller, *Dictionary of Latin and Greek Theological Terms: Drawn Principally from Protestant Scholastic Theology* (Ada: Baker, 1985).

what anyone or everyone else says. If anyone or even everyone else together could tell the believer what to believe, Scripture would not be his sole authority; something else would have binding authority. Thus, according to *sola Scriptura*, any role that Tradition, a Magisterium, Bible commentaries, or anything else may play in theology is simply to suggest interpretations and evidence to the believer as he makes his own decision. Each individual Christian is thus put in the position of being his own theologian.

PRIVATE JUDGMENT

Of course, we all know that the average Christian does not exercise this role in any consistent way, even the average person we might consider to be a genuine, "born again" believer. There are simply too many godly people who are very devout in their faith in Jesus, but who are in no way inclined to become theologians.

Not only are average Christians totally disinclined to fulfill the role of theologian, but if they try to do so, and if they arrive at conclusions different than those of the church to which they belong — an easy task considering the number of different theological issues — then they will quickly discover that their right to private judgment amounts to a right to shut up or leave the congregation. The Reformers, starting with Luther and Calvin, and those who follow in their footsteps, have long realized that, although they must preach the doctrine of private judgment, they must prohibit the exercise of this right in practice for others, to ensure their own right to preach, and to prevent the group from being torn apart by strife. Despite this, the continued exercise of private judgment has resulted in the numerous Protestant denominations and independent churches that we are familiar with today. This disintegration of Christianity into so many competing factions, teaching different doctrines on key theological issues, leads to a myriad of questions. *What kind of faith saves? Is Baptism necessary? Is Baptism for infants? Must Baptism be by immersion only? Can one lose salvation? How? Can it be gotten back? How? Is the Real Presence true? Are spiritual gifts like tongues and healing for today? Are they for everyone? What about predestination? What about free will? What about church government?* These questions are an important indicator of the practical failure of the doctrine of private judgment, and thus the doctrine of *sola Scriptura.* Beyond that indicator, moreover, is a whole set of practical presuppositions that the doctrine of *sola Scriptura* makes, every one of which provides not just an argument against the doctrine, but a fatal blow to it.

The bottom line is this: Was *sola Scriptura* God's plan for Christian theology? Was the idea of *sola Scriptura* even possible before the advent of certain technological developments, which were unknown in the ancient world? If God had intended the individual Christian to use *sola Scriptura* as his operating principle, then it would have to be something the average Christian could implement. We can therefore judge whether *sola Scriptura* could have been God's plan for the individual Christian by asking whether the average Christian in world history could have implemented it. It is in this practical area that the doctrine comes crashing down, for it has a number of presuppositions which are in no way true of the average Christian of world history, and certainly not of the average Christian of early Church history.

PRESUPPOSITION #1

First, if each Christian is to make a thorough study of the Scriptures and decide for himself what they mean (even taking into consideration the interpretations of others), then it follows that he must have a copy of the Scriptures to use in making his thorough study (a non-thorough study being a dangerous thing, as any Protestant apologist will tell you, warning against the cults and their Bible-studying tactics). Thus the universal application of *sola Scriptura* presupposes the mass manufacturing of books, and of the Bible in particular.

This, however, was completely impossible before the invention of the printing press, for without this there could not be enough copies of the Scriptures for individual Christians to use. *Sola Scriptura* therefore presupposes the inventing of the printing press, something that did not happen for the first fourteen hundred years of Church history.

It is often noted by even Protestant historians that the Reformation could not have taken off like it did in the early 1500s if the printing press had not been invented in the mid–1400s. This is more true than they know, because the printing press not only allowed the early Protestants to mass-produce works containing their teachings about what the Bible meant; it also allowed the mass production of the Bible itself (as Catholics were already doing — one does realize, of course, that the Gutenberg Bible and the other versions of the Bible being produced before Protestantism were all Catholic Bibles). Without the ability to mass-produce copies of the Scriptures for individual Christians to interpret, the doctrine of *sola Scriptura* could not function, since one would only have limited access to the texts otherwise — via the Scripture readings at Mass and the costly, hand-made copies of the Bible kept on public display at a local church. Thus, *sola Scriptura* presupposes the printing press.

This is a key reason why the Reformation happened when it did — several decades after the invention of the printing press. It took time for the idea of the printing press to make its mark on the European mind and get people excited about the idea of easily available books. It was in this heady atmosphere, the first time in human history when dozens of ancient works were being mass-produced and sold, that people suddenly got excited with the thought, "Hey! We could give copies of the Bible to everyone! Everyone could read the Scriptures for themselves!" This thought led quickly into *sola Scriptura* in the minds of those who wished to oppose historic Christian theology, as it would provide a justification for their own desire to depart from orthodoxy ("Hey, I read the Scriptures, and this is what they say to me!"). Of course, the invention of the printing press does not itself enable every Christian in the world to have and utilize a copy of the Bible (as all the calls for Bibles to be sent to Russia illustrate), which leads to the next practical presupposition of *sola Scriptura*.

PRESUPPOSITION #2

Second, besides the printing press, *sola Scriptura* also presupposes the universal distribution of books and of the Bible in particular. For it is no good if enough copies of the Bible exist but they can't be gotten into the hands of the average believer. Thus there must be a distribution network capable of delivering affordable copies of the Bible to the average Christian. This is the case today in the developed world. Even today we cannot get enough Bibles into many lands due to economic and political restraints, as the fundraising appeals of Bible societies and their stories of Bible smuggling inform us. However, throughout the great majority of Christian history, the universal distribution of books would have been totally impossible even in what is now the developed world. During most of Church history, the "developed world" was undeveloped.

The political systems, economies, logistical networks, and travel infrastructure that make the mass distribution of Bibles possible today simply did not exist for three–quarters of Church history. There was no way to get the books to the peasants, and no way the peasants could have afforded them in the first place. There just wasn't enough cash in circulation (just try giving a printer five thousand chickens for the thousand Bibles he has just printed — much less keeping the chickens alive and transported from the time the peasants pay them to the time the printer gets them).

PRESUPPOSITION #3

Third, if the average Christian is going to read the Scriptures and decide for himself what they mean, then he obviously must be able to read. Having someone read them to him is not sufficient, not only because the person would only be able to do it occasionally (having a number of people to read to), but also because the person needs to be able to go over the passage multiple times. He must look at its exact wording and grammatical structure, quickly flip to other passages bearing on the topic to formulate the different aspects of a doctrine as he is thinking about it, and finally record his insights so he doesn't forget them and keep the evidence straight in his mind. He therefore must be literate and able to read for himself. Thus *sola Scriptura* presupposes universal literacy.

PRESUPPOSITION #4

Fourth, if the average Christian is going to make a study of what Scripture says and decide what it teaches, he must possess adequate scholarly support material, for he must either be able to read the texts in the original languages or have material capable of telling him when there is a translation question that could affect doctrine. (For example, does the Greek word for "baptize" mean "immerse" or does it have a broader meaning? Does the biblical term for "justify" mean to make righteous in only a legal sense or sometimes in a broader one?) He must also have these scholarly support works (commentaries and such) to suggest to him possible alternate interpretations to evaluate, for no one person is going to be able to think of every interpretive option on every passage of Scripture that is relevant to every major Christian doctrine. No Protestant pastor (at least no pastors who are not in extreme anti-intellectual circles) would dream of formulating his views without such support materials, and he thus cannot expect the average Christian to do so either. Indeed, the average Christian is going to need such support materials even more than a trained pastor. Thus *sola Scriptura* also presupposes the possession — not just the existence — of adequate support materials.

PRESUPPOSITION #5

Fifth, if the average Christian is to do a thorough study of the Bible for himself, then he obviously must have adequate time in which to do this study. If he is working in the fields or at home (or, later, in the factory) for ten, twelve, fifteen, or eighteen hours a day, he obviously doesn't have time to do this, especially not in addition to the care and raising of his family and his own need to eat, sleep, and recreate. Not even a Sunday rest will provide him with the adequate time, for nobody becomes adept in the Bible just by reading the Bible on Sundays — as Protestants stress to their own members when encouraging daily Bible reading. Thus *sola Scriptura* presupposes the universal possession of adequate leisure time in which to make a thorough study of the Bible for oneself.

PRESUPPOSITION #6

Sixth, if the average Christian is going to evaluate competing interpretations for himself then he must have a significant amount of skill in evaluating arguments. He must be able to recognize what is a good argument and what is not, what is a fallacy and what is not, what counts as evidence and what does not. That is quite a bit of critical-thinking skill, and, as anyone who has tried to teach basic, introductory logic to college students or has tried to read and grade the persuasive essays they write for philosophy tests can tell you, that level of critical thinking often does not exist in the average, literate, modern college student, much less the average, illiterate, medieval peasant. This is especially true when it comes to the abstract concepts and truth claims involved in philosophy and theology. Thus *sola Scriptura* also presupposes a high level of universal education in critical-thinking skills (a level which does not exist even today).

PRESUPPOSITION #7

Unless the faithful are to undertake the very challenging task of learning biblical Greek, Hebrew, and Aramaic, they also will need accurate and trustworthy translations of the Bible in the language they speak. This is more challenging than it may appear. All translations experience a degree of bias due to the theological commitments of the translators, and sometimes this bias is extreme (as when groups like the Jehovah's Witnesses produce flatly erroneous Bible translations to support their views). Additionally, many editions of the Bible contain introductions, footnotes, and other materials that advocate the publishers' views (which contradict those expressed in other editions and that may even seek to undermine the biblical text). With the bewildering array of translations and editions available today, the average reader is confronted with a challenging problem if he is to do theology by Scripture alone.

SUMMARY OF PRESUPPOSITIONS

Therefore, *sola Scriptura* presupposes (1) the existence of the printing press, (2) the universal distribution of Bibles, (3) universal literacy, (4) the universal possession of scholarly support materials, (5) the universal possession of adequate time for study, (6) a universal education in a high level of critical-thinking skills, and (7) accurate and trustworthy translations. Needless to say, this group of conditions was not true in the crucial early centuries of the Church, was not true throughout the main course of Church history, and is not even true today. The nonexistence of the printing press alone means *sola Scriptura* was totally unthinkable for almost three–quarters of Christian history! All of this is besides the limitations we mentioned earlier: the fact that the average Christian, even the average devout Christian, has no inclination whatsoever to conduct the kind of Bible study needed to become his own theologian, and the fact that he is encouraged by many pressures from his own pastor and congregation (including the threat of being cast out) to fall in line and not challenge — especially publicly challenge — the party platform.

CHRISTIANITY FOR THE COMMON MAN?

It is thus hard to think of *sola Scriptura* as anything but the theory spawned by a bunch of idealistic, Renaissance-era dilettantes — people who had an interest in being their own theologians, who had a classical education in critical-thinking skills, who had enough leisure time for study, who had plenty of scholarly support materials, who had good reading skills, who had access to Bible-sellers, and most importantly, who had printed Bibles!

The average Christian today, even the average Christian in the developed world, does not fit that profile, and the average Christian in world history certainly did not, much less the average Christian in the early centuries. What this means, since God does not ask a person to do what they are incapable of doing, is that God does not expect the average Christian of world history to use *sola Scriptura*. He expects the average

Christian to obtain and maintain his knowledge of theology in some other way.

But if God expects the average Christian to obtain and maintain the Christian Faith without using *sola Scriptura*, then *sola Scriptura* cannot be God's plan.

JIMMY AKIN *is an internationally known author and speaker. As the senior apologist at Catholic Answers, he has more than twenty years of experience in defending and explaining the Catholic Faith. Jimmy is a convert to the Catholic Faith and has an extensive background in the Bible, theology, the Church Fathers, philosophy, canon law, and liturgy. Jimmy is a weekly guest on the national radio program* Catholic Answers Live, *a regular contributor to* Catholic Answers Magazine, *and a popular blogger and podcaster. His personal website is JimmyAkin.com.*

THE PERSPICUITY ("CLEARNESS") OF SCRIPTURE[4]

DAVE ARMSTRONG

A key aspect of the historical Reformed understanding of sola Scriptura *— though often forgotten or ignored today — is the perspicuity or clearness of Scripture. Martin Luther stated the classic Protestant understanding of this in his own favorite (and arguably most important) writing,* The Bondage of the Will*:*

> All the things, therefore, contained in the Scriptures, are made manifest, although some places, from the words not being understood, are yet obscure ... And, if the words are obscure in one place, yet they are clear in another ... For Christ has opened our understanding to understand the Scriptures ...

> But, if many things still remain abstruse to many, this does not arise from obscurity in the Scriptures, but from their own blindness or want of understanding, who do not go the way to see the all-perfect clearness of the truth ... Let, therefore, wretched men cease to impute, with blasphemous perverseness, the darkness and obscurity of their own heart to the all-clear scriptures of God ...

---

4   This is a revised version of an article written by Dave Armstrong that was previously published in the Coming Home Network International's *Sola Scriptura* journal. Reprinted with permission.

> If you speak of the internal clearness, no man sees one iota in the Scriptures, but he that hath the Spirit of God … If you speak of the external clearness, nothing whatever is left obscure or ambiguous; but all things that are in the Scriptures, are by the Word brought forth into the clearest light, and proclaimed to the whole world.[5]

Most Evangelical Protestants agree with Luther's sentiments above, either entirely or mostly, and hold to the view that — when all is said and done — the Bible is basically *perspicuous* (clearly understandable) in and of itself, without the absolute *necessity* for theological teaching, scholarly interpretation, and the authority of the Church (however defined).

This is not to say that Protestants are consciously taught to ignore Christian historical precedent altogether and shun theological instruction — although, sadly, the tendency of ahistoricism and anti-intellectualism is strong in many circles.

But as noted in Luther's argument above, even given perspicuity, not all Bible-believing Christians agree on the content and meaning of Scripture. The argument expressed by Luther to explain these differences is what might be called the "sin" explanation. The Bible is indeed more often than not quite clear when approached open-mindedly and with a moral willingness to accept its teachings, but many Christians arrive at contradictory, yet sincerely held convictions. Scripture itself teaches, however, that error is necessarily present wherever disagreements exist — clearly not a desirable situation, as all falsehood is harmful (for example, Jn 8:44, 16:13; 2 Thess 2:10–12; 1 Jn 4:6). Is it just, though, to invoke "sin" as the all-encompassing reason for these Christian disagreements (as

---

5 Martin Luther, *The Bondage of the Will*, trans. Henry Cole (Grand Rapids: Baker Book House, 1976), pp. 25–27, 29.

Luther typically does), or is this only absurdly simplistic, if not also uncharitable and judgmental?

MERELY SECONDARY ISSUES

A more common explanation for the wide variety of opinions is that Christians and denominations differ mostly over *secondary* issues, not *fundamental* or *central* doctrines. Perspicuity is usually said to apply primarily to those doctrines that are "essential" for salvation. Accordingly, it follows that whatever is necessary for salvation can be found in the Bible by any literate individual without the requisite assistance of an ecclesiastical body. This is presupposed in, for example, the widespread practice of passing out Bibles to the newly evangelized, oftentimes with no provision made for further guidance and supervision.

Right from the beginning, however, the Protestant Reformers disagreed over the meaning of many things that had previously been considered essential. For example, Zwingli and Oecolampadius, two lesser Reformers, differed with Luther on how to understand the Real Presence of Christ in the Eucharist, while the Anabaptists dissented completely on the Eucharist, infant Baptism, ordination, and the function of civil authority. Luther regarded these fellow Protestants as "damned" and "out of the Church" for these reasons. Reformers John Calvin and Martin Bucer held to a third position on the Eucharist (broadly speaking), intermediate between Luther's Real Presence (*consubstantiation*) and Zwingli's purely symbolic belief. By 1577, a book entitled *200 Interpretations of the Words, "This is My Body"* was published in Ingolstadt, Germany.

Over time, this wide range of irreconcilable differences led many Protestants to maintain that the Eucharist and Baptism are neither primary nor essential doctrines (which is curious, since these are the two sacraments accepted by the majority of

Protestants). Jesus, however, said: "Unless you eat the flesh of the Son of man and drink his blood, you have no life in you" (Jn 6:53). This certainly sounds essential, even to the extent that a man's salvation might be in jeopardy. St. Paul, too, regarded communion with equally great seriousness and of the utmost importance to one's spiritual well being and relationship with Jesus Christ (1 Cor 10:14–22, 11:23–30). Thus we are already in the realm of salvation — a primary doctrine. Lutherans and many Anglicans (for example, the Oxford *Tractarians* and C.S. Lewis) believe in the Real Presence, whereas most Evangelicals do not, yet this is not considered cause for alarm or even discomfort.

SOTERIOLOGY

Protestants also differ on other *soteriological* issues. Most Methodists, Anglicans, Lutherans, Pentecostals, some Baptists, many non-denominationalists, and other groups are Arminian in theology: they accept *free will* and the possibility of falling away from salvation (*apostasy*). On the other hand, Presbyterians, Reformed, a few Baptist denominations, and other groups are Calvinist in theology: they deny free will and the possibility of apostasy for the *elect*. In contrast to the former denominations, the latter groups have a stronger view of the nature of *original sin*, and deny that the atonement is *universal*.

Traditional, orthodox Methodism (following founder John Wesley) and many "high church" Anglicans have had views of *sanctification* (that is, the relationship of faith and works, and of God's enabling and preceding grace and man's cooperation) akin to that of Catholicism. These are questions of how one repents and is saved (justification) and of what is required afterward to either manifest or maintain this salvation (sanctification and perseverance). Thus, they are primary doctrines, even by Protestant criteria.

BAPTISM

The same state of affairs is true concerning Baptism, where Protestants are split into infant and adult camps. Furthermore, the infant camp contains those who accept baptismal regeneration (Lutherans, Anglicans, and to some extent, Methodists), as does the adult camp (Churches of Christ and Disciples of Christ). They believe regeneration absolutely has a bearing on salvation, and therefore is a primary doctrine. The Salvation Army and the Quakers don't baptize at all (and neither celebrate the Eucharist). Thus, there are five distinct competing belief-systems among Protestants with regard to Baptism.

Scripture seems to clearly refer to baptismal regeneration in Acts 2:38 (forgiveness of sins), 22:16 (wash away your sins), Romans 6:3–4, 1 Corinthians 6:11, Titus 3:5 (he saved us ... by the washing of regeneration), and other passages. For this reason, many prominent Protestant individuals and denominations have held to the position of baptismal regeneration, which is anathema to the Baptist/Presbyterian/Reformed branch of Protestantism — the predominant Evangelical outlook at present. We need look no further than Martin Luther himself — from whom all Protestants inherit their understanding of both *sola Scriptura* and *faith alone* (*sola fide*) as the prerequisites for salvation and justification — who largely agrees with the Catholic position on sacramental and regenerative infant Baptism:

> Little children ... are free in every way, secure and saved solely through the glory of their baptism ... Through the prayer of the believing church which presents it ... the infant is changed, cleansed, and renewed by inpoured faith. Nor should I doubt that even a godless adult could be changed, in any of the sacraments, if the same church prayed for and presented him, as we read of the paralytic in

the Gospel, who was healed through the faith of others (Mark 2:3–12). I should be ready to admit that in this sense the sacraments of the New Law are efficacious in conferring grace, not only to those who do not, but even to those who do most obstinately present an obstacle.[6]

Likewise, in his *Large Catechism* (1529), Luther writes:

Expressed in the simplest form, the power, the effect, the benefit, the fruit, and the purpose of baptism is to save. No one is baptized that he may become a prince, but, as the words declare [of Mark 16:16], that he may be saved. But to be saved, we know very well, is to be delivered from sin, death, and Satan, and to enter Christ's kingdom and live forever with him … Through the Word, baptism receives the power to become the washing of regeneration, as St. Paul calls it in Titus 3:5 … Faith clings to the water and believes it to be baptism which effects pure salvation and life …

When sin and conscience oppress us … you may say: It is a fact that I am baptized, but, being baptized, I have the promise that I shall be saved and obtain eternal life for both soul and body …Hence, no greater jewel can adorn our body or soul than baptism; for through it perfect holiness and salvation become accessible to us.[7]

Anglicanism concurs with Luther on this matter. Article 27 on Baptism in its authoritative *Thirty-Nine Articles* reads as follows:

6   Martin Luther, *The Babylonian Captivity of the Church*, 1520, trans. A.T.W. Steinhauser, rev. ed. (Philadelphia: Fortress Press, 1970), p. 197.

7   Martin Luther, *Large Catechism* (Minneapolis: Augsburg Publishing House, 1935), sections 223–24, 230, pp. 162, 165.

Baptism is not only a sign of profession, and mark of difference, whereby Christian men are discerned from others that be not christened, but it is also a sign of Regeneration or New-Birth, whereby, as by an instrument, they that receive Baptism rightly are grafted into the Church; the promises of the forgiveness of sin, and of our adoption to be the sons of God by the Holy Ghost, are visibly signed and sealed; Faith is confirmed, and Grace increased by virtue of prayer unto God.

The Baptism of young Children is in any wise to be retained in the Church, as most agreeable with the institution of Christ.[8]

The venerable John Wesley, founder of Methodism, who is widely admired by Protestants and Catholics alike, agreed, too, that children are regenerated (and justified initially) by means of infant Baptism. From this position he never wavered. In his *Articles of Religion* (1784), which is a revised version of the Anglican *Articles*, he retains an abridged form of the clause on Baptism, stating that it is "a sign of regeneration, or the new birth."[9]

AN IRRESOLVABLE DILEMMA

These doctrinal disputes, particularly that over the doctrine of Baptism, illustrate the irresolvable Protestant dilemma with regard to the *perspicuity* of Scripture. Again, the Bible is obviously not perspicuous enough to efficiently eliminate these differences, unless one arrogantly maintains that sin always blinds those in the opposing camps from seeing obvious truths, which even a "plowboy" (Luther's famous phrase)

---

8   "Of Baptism," Article 27 in *The Book of Common Prayer* (1563, language revised 1801; New York: The Seabury Press, 1979), p. 873.

9   John Wesley, *Articles of Religion*, no. 17.

ought to be able to grasp. Obviously, an authoritative (and even infallible) interpreter is needed whether or not the Bible is perspicuous enough to be theoretically understood without help. Nothing could be clearer than that. *Paper infallibility* is no substitute for conciliar and/or *papal infallibility*, or at least an authoritative denominational (creedal/confessional) authority, if nothing else.

The conclusion is inescapable: either biblical perspicuity is a falsehood or one or more of the doctrines of regeneration, justification, sanctification, salvation, election, free will, predestination, perseverance, eternal security, the atonement, original sin, the Eucharist, Baptism, all "five points" of Calvinism (TULIP), and issues affecting the very *gospel* itself — are not *central*. A sincere Christian cannot have it both ways.

To say it a different way: people like Martin Luther (due to his beliefs in the Real Presence and baptismal regeneration), John Wesley, C.S. Lewis, and entire denominations such as Methodists, Anglicans, Lutherans, Churches of Christ, various Pentecostal groups, and the Salvation Army should be read out of the Christian Faith due to their "unorthodoxy," as defined by the Evangelicals, such as Baptists, Presbyterians, and Reformed (even so, the last two groups baptize infants, although they vehemently deny that this causes regeneration, whereas Baptists don't). Since most Protestants are unwilling to *anathematize* other Protestants, perspicuity dissolves into a boiling cauldron of incomprehensible contradictions, and as such, must be discarded or at the very least seriously reformulated in order to harmonize with the Bible and logic.

What generally happens is that Protestant freedom of conscience is valued more than unity and the certainty of doctrinal truth in all matters (not just the core issues alone). The inquirer with newfound zeal for Christ is in trouble if he expects to easily attain any comprehensive certainty within Protestantism. All he can do is take a "head count" of scholars, pastors, evangelists, and *Bible Dictionaries* and see who lines up where on the various sides of the numerous disagreements. Or else he can just uncritically accept the word of whatever denomination with which he is associated. Whichever procedure he chooses, however well intentioned, is essentially arbitrary and sadly destined to produce further confusion.

The Scriptures are, indeed, the inspired Word of God, written by human authors under the inspiration of the Holy Spirit. But history demonstrates that it could hardly have been God's plan for this book to be the sole foundation of truth, or that alone it is so clear that it is without need of interpretation. For this, God gave us a trustworthy teacher.

DAVE ARMSTRONG *is a full-time Catholic apologist and evangelist who has defended Catholicism for twenty-five years. Formerly a Protestant campus missionary, Armstrong entered the Catholic Church in 1991. He has written forty-nine books, as well as articles for many Catholic periodicals. He, his wife, Judy, and their four children live near Detroit, Michigan. His website,* Biblical Evidence for Catholicism, *is hosted at the Patheos supersite: http://www.patheos.com/blogs/davearmstrong/. Some of the books David has authored include:* A Biblical Defense of Catholicism, Proving the Catholic Faith Is Biblical, *and* The One-Minute Apologist. *He is co-author of the apologetics inserts of* The New Catholic Answer Bible, *published by Our Sunday Visitor.*

3

"PASTOR, CAN I ASK YOU SOMETHING?"[10]

MARCUS GRODI

So far, we have addressed the perspicuity of Scripture and whether the idea of sola Scriptura *was even feasible in the early days of the Church, given the lack of necessary technologies and conditions, which didn't arise until the late fifteenth century. If God desires all to be saved and the gospel to spread to the ends of the earth, is it conceivable that He would have limited this outreach to the availability of the written page?*

The question arises, therefore, whether the Scriptures themselves teach sola Scriptura. *We'll address this question in the next few chapters, but I'd like to introduce this topic with the following scenario. It's based on true events that occurred in my life and the lives of others I've interviewed, but has been brought together in this fictional scene from my novel* How Firm a Foundation. *In the dialogue, the pastor outlines the typical biblical proofs used to argue that the Bible teaches* sola Scriptura.

Those of you who are pastors know from experience your need to steel yourself — to batten down the hatches and get the women and children below — whenever certain parishioners begin a

---

10 This contains an excerpt from a novel, *How Firm a Foundation*, by Marcus Grodi (Zanesville: CHResources, 2011), pp. 133–45, passim.

question with these seemingly innocent words, "Pastor, can I ask you something?" The following is just such an experience.

The scene takes place at the monthly board meeting of Respite Congregational Church. The recently hired Reverend Stephen LaPointe has just conveyed his plans for the upcoming new members' classes, when a concerned board member interrupts him.

"Pastor, may I ask something?" Larry Howe said. "I'm reluctant to do so in front of this peanut gallery, but something's been bugging me ever since we joined this church."

Fighting through guffaws all around, Larry quipped, holding up his arms in the form of a cross, "All right, all right, back off."

The board quieted down, anxious to hear what sticky conundrum Larry might pose this time.

"As you know, my wife and I used to be Roman Catholics, and thank God we're here now." Larry gave a demonstrative sigh of relief, which he knew everyone would understand. "Ever since our conversion, Sue and I have become avid Bible readers. We're not Bible scholars by any means, so don't get me wrong, but let's just say I've read the Bible more in the last ten years than in the entire first thirty years of my life. Now, one of the main tenets that separates us Protestants from Catholics is that we believe that the Bible *alone* is the sole foundation for our faith, correct?"

"Yes," Stephen responded, hoping this would pass quickly. "Most Protestants hold to *sola Scriptura*, though there is great diversity as to how this is understood and applied. You also realize that many Congregationalists no longer believe this. Nevertheless, that is at least what we believe here at Respite."

"Fine. So if I get this straight, this inspired book," Larry said, raising the leather Revised Standard Bible that always accompanied him to church, "is the sole foundation for all that we must believe and practice, especially for our salvation?"

"Yes, that's true." Uncertain where this was leading, Stephen nevertheless anticipated nothing he could not answer.

"Then two things that, as I said, have been bothering me. First, if the Bible is the sole foundation for our faith, then where does the Bible say this specifically? I mean, for something this important and foundational, you'd think it would be stated clearly?"

Invariably, Stephen had to explain this to every new members' class, so he knew immediately where to turn. "This is most clearly affirmed in 2 Timothy 3:16 and 17. Here, pass me your Bible, I forgot mine tonight."

This brought the expected sniggers.

"'All Scripture is inspired by God and profitable for teaching,'" Stephen read, "'for reproof, for correction, and for training in righteousness, that the man of God may be complete, equipped for every good work.'"

Recalling what he had learned from his old theology professor, Stephen added, "An alternate way to translate the Greek term, given here as '*profitable*,' is '*sufficient*.' All Scripture is therefore inspired and sufficient for teaching, et cetera.

"There are other verses that solidify our belief in the Bible's sufficiency, especially where Jesus quotes the Old Testament as authoritative, and where New Testament authors discourage believers from relying on the traditions of men. In Hebrews 4:12, for example. 'For the word of God is living and active, sharper than any two–edged sword,'" Stephen read, gesticulating with the Bible to emphasize that it was this book to which the author was referring. "From this and other passages, we conclude that the Bible is God's gift to His people, who under the guidance of the Holy Spirit are led into all truth."

"Then you would say, therefore," Larry responded, "that the Bible is the pillar and bulwark of the truth?"

"Yes, that is a good way to put it," Stephen said, pleased with the clarity of this ardent church member.

"Then, why does the Bible itself claim something different?" Larry asked with a sly smile. "Please explain 1 Timothy 3:15."

Stephen paged back, curious about Larry's reference. Stephen had read through the entire New Testament many times, so he was anticipating no surprises. Like most Evangelical pastors, he had memorized the most significant verses and had a basic mental image of the rest, but this particular text did not ring a bell.

Locating the page in Larry's Bible, he thumbed down to the reference, finding that Larry had underlined this text. A question mark with an exclamation point had been added in the margin. Stephen scanned the verse silently, but it wasn't until he began reading it aloud that the significance of Larry's question struck him.

Stephen's pace slowed as he pronounced each word more cautiously and pensively. Once finished, he sat silently, marveling that he had failed to notice this passage before. In his own Bible, he had underlined the preceding passages about the duties of bishops and deacons, and the subsequent passage containing one of the oldest Christian creeds. But Stephen was dumbfounded.

Why have I never seen this before? And how do I explain it to Larry and the board?

And Larry and the board waited, bewildered by Stephen's awkward silence.

Stephen gathered his thoughts.

"The problem with interpreting texts like this, especially when we compare a verse from one New Testament book with that from another, is that it's impossible to understand fully what these first–century writers meant by their terms — especially now, nearly two thousand years later. When Paul wrote here that 'the church of the living God' is 'the pillar and bulwark of the truth,' he had no inkling what the word *church* would come to mean over the centuries. He surely could not have predicted how church leaders would wrestle with one another for control of the expanding Church, or how the Roman Emperor Constantine would eventually settle the whole mess by declaring Christianity the official religion of the Roman people and the bishop of Rome the head of the Church. Paul could not have anticipated that this term would one day be used to describe the corrupt hierarchy of popes, bishops, and priests. Nor could he have foreseen the Reformation that God would initiate to correct this. Finally, Paul with his limited vision of the world could never have imagined the thousands of Christian groups that now call themselves churches.

"Paul certainly must have meant what we believe today," Stephen continued, though a voice from within prodded, *But who do you mean by "we"?*

"The Church is not physical structures or hierarchies of bishops, or even some collective list of members' names from all the world's churches. No, the Church is the invisible body of believers encircling the globe — past, present, and future — in whom the Holy Spirit dwells by grace through faith, and therefore where God's Word and God's truth are rightly interpreted, taught, and believed."

Satisfied that he had temporarily dodged this bullet, Stephen scanned the faces of his board for signs of concurrence. He had given them essentially his pat summary of the New Testament authors' understanding of the term *church* — he only hoped it sat better with the board than it was sitting in his own conscience. The majority nodded with smiles of support, except Larry.

"But Pastor," he asked, "how can a worldwide, invisible, and unorganized assortment of believers be a pillar and foundation of truth? I have friends in other churches who love Jesus and His Word, yet believe differently than I do. Which of us is speaking for this invisible Church?"

Stephen studied the man's rough face. Larry managed his family-owned logging company, and his complexion and demeanor had been hewn by many long days outside in the New Hampshire winters.

"The things that are essential, we are to agree on; it's the nonessentials that divide us," Stephen replied with force.

"So you're saying that issues like how or when a person is baptized, or whether the Lord's Supper is truly the Body and Blood of Jesus or just a powerless symbol, or whether abortion is murder, or whether salvation can be lost or is eternally secure, or whether one adheres to the traditional creeds — all of these are nonessentials?"

Stephen felt like one of the Pharisees Jesus had reasoned into a corner, because regardless of whether he said "yes" or "no," he would invite the ire of any number of board members. *Thanks, Larry,* he grumbled inwardly. *I really needed this tonight.*

"What we are called to consider true are those things that have been believed quasi-unanimously by all Christians, at all times and in all places," again quoting an answer his old theology professor had once given to a similar question. "The unfortunate conflict between Christian believers stems from ignorance, pride, sin, or the denial of how the Spirit has led Christians from the beginning. We are Congregationalists because we believe that we are preserving the freedoms as expressed by Paul and the other New Testament writers."

Larry was poised with a response, but Stephen continued quickly: "Larry, it's getting late, and besides, I don't think I can completely satisfy your question tonight. If you'd like, we can continue this another time."

"Thank you, Pastor. That would be helpful," Larry said reluctantly.

Stephen rose and offered him back his Bible, but for what seemed like an eternity they played tug of war as Stephen held on, anxious to read that verse again. Confused, Larry released his grip. Embarrassed, Stephen did the same, and the Bible fell loudly to the floor.

"I'm sorry, Larry," Stephen said, bending meekly to retrieve it. He then gave it freely to its owner. Evading the ensuing awkwardness, Stephen turned his attention back to George, "That's really all I've got for tonight. If you have questions about the resources on the table, please let me know."

Stephen sat down relieved, but that verse continued to disturb him.

Anxious to refocus the board's attention, George stood and announced, "Let's move on to the last sticky wicket of our agenda: are we as a church going to take part in this year's ecumenical Good Friday service, scheduled to take place at St. Anne's Catholic Parish?"

As the board debated the ecumenical issue, Stephen remained unengaged. In the end, the ecumenists won out, stressing that any relationships established with the members of St. Anne's Parish would only lead to movement towards Respite Congregational, and not the other way around.

The roadside diner was crowded with truckers. The only available booth was an uncleared one in the smoking section, but Stephen took it anyway. He still had another seventy miles to drive, but he could ignore the nagging curiosity no longer.

"What'll you have?" asked an aging, don't-mess-with-me waitress. She cleared the table, wiping it clean with a sopping rag.

He waited for her to finish.

"What do you want?" she demanded again, in a voice that invited the stares of several truckers. Stephen noticed immediately that their sympathies were not with him.

He raised his hands in bewilderment.

With a look of incredulity to a burly customer in the next booth, she pointed to a small crumpled menu behind the usual collection of condiments.

After a quick scan of the options, Stephen said, "A black coffee and a number six, eggs over easy."

She turned away towards the kitchen, with no sign of acknowledgment.

But no matter. Stopping for breakfast was only an excuse. Ever since the board meeting, Stephen had been frantic to re-examine the Scriptures and the answers he had given to Larry's questions — which Larry and he both knew were unsatisfactory.

"You did say black?" the waitress said, as she placed a coffee and a greasy number six before him.

"Yes," but she was already gone.

The overcooked eggs, limp bacon, and cold toast looked only marginally palatable, so after a few token bites, he pushed the plate aside. From his briefcase, he removed his Greek-English New Testament. Even if it took all morning, he was determined to get to the bottom of those verses in First Timothy, for he recognized the underlying significance in Larry's question.

First he pleaded for the Spirit's guidance, then reread the verses that until last night he had failed to see: "I hope to come to you soon, but I am writing these instructions to you so that, if I am delayed, you may know how one ought to behave in the household of God, which is the church of the living God, the pillar and bulwark of the truth."

Free from the scrutiny of Larry and the board, Stephen noted, first, that Paul had written this letter as a precautionary measure. Paul was planning to visit with Timothy, but in the event that his plans might fall through, he had penned this letter to pass along instructions on how people ought to behave as Christians.

In other words, Paul's preferred means of teaching Timothy was face-to-face.

Stephen sipped the black, keep-you-awake-all-night coffee and silently thanked the Holy Spirit for the delay nearly two thousand years ago that had forced Paul to write this letter. Otherwise, the world might never have seen these instructions.

Reflecting further, Stephen envisioned the imprisoned Apostle sitting hunched over a wooden table under the dim glow of an oil lamp. He was writing with a sharpened feather quill on a yellow roll of papyrus. This picture then faded into an image of Paul sitting more casually across a table from young Timothy. The two friends were laughing and sharing chalices of wine — for wasn't this Paul's advice near the end of this same letter? As Stephen considered this, he thought, *Wouldn't Paul have said a whole lot more to Timothy face-to-face than he was able to write on that small papyrus? Did Paul summarize everything that was necessary in this short letter, or was this merely a quick introduction to the more detailed list of things he wanted to deliver in person?*

Stephen turned to Paul's Second Letter to Timothy and reread the verse that he had assumed would answer Larry's challenge.

All Scripture, Stephen thought. *All Scripture? When Timothy received this letter, what would he have understood Paul to mean by this? Would he have considered Paul's letter itself as "Scripture," or only a casual, yet important letter from his father in the faith? What would Timothy and Paul have considered Scripture?*

"Anything else?" the waitress asked, removing his unfinished breakfast and slapping down the bill.

"Some more coffee, please."

"Hey, this ain't a library," she said, filling his cup to a positive meniscus.

Stephen started to respond, but again, she was gone.

When Paul wrote this, he thought, *returning to the text, the New Testament as we know it had not been collected. In fact, we're not even sure whether the Gospels had been written yet. Therefore, the only thing Paul could have referred to as Scripture was the Old Testament — which of course at the time wouldn't have been called that, but "the Law and the Prophets."*

And also, he continued, *we know from the way the New Testament writers quoted the Old Testament that they used the Greek translation, called the Septuagint. So the term "Scripture" here must literally mean the Greek Old Testament.*

He glanced down the page to the footnotes. A chain reference pointed to another of Paul's letters. He casually flipped back to 2 Thessalonians 2:15. He leaned back to stretch as he began reading, his mind focused on his previous thoughts, until what he read shot him forward in the booth: "So then, brethren, stand firm and hold to the traditions which you were taught by us, either by word of mouth or by letter."

He read this again, and then again. As he did, the two mental pictures of Paul writing and of Paul teaching Timothy face-to-face melded into a composite that represented in his mind how the Christian faith was passed on from Jesus to Apostle to local preacher to the people: by word of mouth and by writing.

Stephen mulled this over, thinking about all three verses at once, and envisioned their interrelationship: the faith of these early Christians was built on the foundation of the Old Testament Scriptures — the Law and the Prophets. But what was written in them needed to be applied to their new situation in Christ — the ancient prophetic references to the coming Messiah needed to be explained so that they could be understood in reference to Jesus. This was what Jesus had explained to the two disciples on the road to Emmaus, and what then was passed on through the Apostle's teachings, both orally and in writing.

Stephen paused as he sensed his thoughts reaching a conclusion. *And if Paul asserts that more was communicated in his sermons and public teaching than he was able to record in his few, short New Testament letters, then, therefore, how can it be accurate to conclude that only what is in Scripture is essential? Paul said that we should hold to the traditions taught orally as well as in writing.*

Traditions.

This word, which he as a Congregationalist rarely used, jumped out at him. Paul was telling these early Christians to hold to traditions taught not only in his letters but also orally.

With apprehension, Stephen followed another chain reference, 1 Corinthians 11:2: "I commend you because you remember me in everything and maintain the traditions even as I have delivered them to you."

"Traditions again," he muttered, "that he 'delivered.'" *I've always presumed that this referred to the written records of Jesus' deeds and words. But why?*

Frantically he followed another reference in the same letter, 4:17, "Therefore I sent to you Timothy ... to remind you of my ways in Christ, as I teach them everywhere in every church."

Teach them everywhere in every church. *Again,* Stephen thought, *Paul's normal way of communicating Christian truth. And in this instance, he sent Timothy instead of a letter.*

Another reference came to mind, and this time he knew the verse by memory, 2 Timothy 2:2, "What you have heard from me before many witnesses entrust to faithful men who will be able to teach others also."

From Jesus to Paul to Timothy to faithful men to others. All through oral teaching without any mandate to write it down or to "look it up in the Bible."

Stephen finished his coffee as his mind raced ahead into what for him was uncharted territory. He turned back to the text in Second Timothy that he had always used to defend *sola Scriptura,* and began reading the verses that immediately preceded it: "But as for you, continue in what you have learned and have firmly believed, knowing from whom you learned it ..."

For Timothy this, therefore, meant from Paul, or his parents, or others, Stephen thought, *not from some as yet uncollected New Testament letters or gospels.*

"... and how from childhood you have been acquainted with the sacred writings ..."

... which had to be the Old Testament Scriptures. But had he actually read these? Possibly not. He was acquainted with these primarily through public readings, probably in the local synagogue and church gatherings. In every way, therefore, he was dependent upon oral teaching.

"... which are able to instruct you for salvation through faith in Christ Jesus."

But the Old Testament is not that clear about how one is saved through faith in Jesus Christ — one needs the New Testament to fully understand this. So if Timothy and the other early Christians didn't have a written New Testament yet, how could they know how to interpret the Old Testament correctly and adequately to lead them to Jesus?

As Stephen asked himself these questions, he casually flipped back to the initial text in First Timothy: "… the church of the living God, the pillar and bulwark of the truth."

"Hey, buddy."

Startled, Stephen broke from his reflection. Hovering over him was a man wearing a soiled apron over a white tee shirt rolled up at the sleeves.

"Take your reading elsewhere. This ain't first period study hall. I've got regular customers waiting to be seated."

"I'm sorry. I was just reading while I finished my coffee."

"Well, finish it in your car."

The man stood aside as Stephen collected his things, threw down a five to cover the bill and tip, and left.

Once by his aging Fairmont, Stephen glanced back through the diner window in time to see the man laughing with several of the customers, mimicking Stephen's studiousness.

Anger rose within Stephen, but realizing that any retaliation to their ridicule was pointless, he merely turned away and threw his briefcase onto the backseat. As he headed off toward Jamesfield, his mind returned to where his reflections had left off.

The Church … the pillar … the bulwark … the truth.

Stephen envisioned Timothy attempting to convince pagan neighbors to believe in Jesus. If they answered back, "Why should we believe this lunacy," then what could Timothy have said? If he had said, "Because the Scriptures say so," he could only have meant the Old Testament, and we know from the experience of the Ethiopian eunuch in Acts that just reading the Old Testament wasn't enough. Timothy would have had to convince them through the witness of those who had seen

Jesus alive after His death on the Cross. But where was this to be found?

The Church ... the pillar ... the bulwark ... the truth.

MARCUS GRODI *is the founder and president of the Coming Home Network International, a lay Catholic apostolate whose mission is helping Protestant clergy and laity come home to the Catholic Church. Marcus is also the host of* The Journey Home *program on EWTN.*

4

THE ILLOGICAL LOGIC
OF *SOLA SCRIPTURA*[11]

MARCUS GRODI

So the question arises, as pondered in the scenario of the last chapter: Does the Bible teach sola Scriptura? On a certain Internet website, this proposal is defended, but with, what I consider, illogical logic. Allow me to explain.

There is a television commercial, selling a certain satellite service, that uses a tongue-in-cheek form of illogical chain logic. The writers presume that we understand not to take their logic seriously, but they also presume that the humor of it will leave us with a positive view of their product.

The logic goes something like this:

1. (Not having our product) might leave one feeling empty.

2. Feeling empty makes one want to feel full.

3. Wanting to feel full makes one eat too much.

4. Eating too much makes one burst out of one's clothing.

5. Bursting out of one's clothing leaves one naked in the street.

6. Standing naked in the street leads to getting arrested.

7. Getting arrested for standing naked in the street puts one in jail.

---

11 This is a revised version of an article written by Marcus Grodi that was originally published in the Coming Home Network International's September 2013 newsletter.

8. Being put in jail for standing naked in the street gives one a strange reputation with your cellmates.

9. If you don't want to have a strange reputation with your cellmates, then you need to buy our product.

It's easy to follow the humor of this illogical logic, but it's not always humorous when this kind of logic is used to interpret Scripture. For example, consider the following flow of logic in an article posted online entitled "A Defense of *Sola Scriptura*":[12]

The first question the authors address is, "Does the Bible Teach *Sola Scriptura*?" and, step by step, here is their logic:

1. Two points must be made concerning whether the Bible teaches sola Scriptura. First, as Catholic scholars themselves recognize, it is not necessary that the Bible explicitly and formally teach *sola Scriptura* in order for this doctrine to be true.

2. Many Christian teachings are a necessary logical deduction of what is clearly taught in the Bible (e.g., the Trinity).

3. Likewise, it is possible that sola Scriptura could be a necessary logical deduction from what is taught in Scripture.

4. Second, the Bible does teach implicitly and logically, if not formally and explicitly, that the Bible alone is the only infallible basis for faith and practice. This it does in a number of ways.

5. One, the fact that Scripture, without tradition, is said to be "God-breathed" (*theopnuestos*) and thus by it believers are "competent, equipped for every good work" (2 Tim 3:16–17 NABRE) supports the doctrine of *sola Scriptura*.

---

12 Norman Geisler and Ralph MacKenzie, "A Defense of Sola Scriptura," Christian Research Institute, http://www.equip.org/articles/a-defense-of-sola-scriptura.

6. This flies in the face of the Catholic claim that the Bible is formally insufficient without the aid of tradition.

7. St. Paul declares that the God-breathed writings are sufficient.

8. And contrary to some Catholic apologists, limiting this to only the Old Testament will not help the Catholic cause for two reasons: first, the New Testament is also called "Scripture" (2 Pet 3:15–16; 1 Tim 5:18; cf. Lk 10:7); second, it is inconsistent to argue that God-breathed writings in the Old Testament are sufficient, but the inspired writings of the New Testament are not.

Though their logic sounds like it works, it's really more like the illogical logic in that commercial. (I can't point fingers, because this is the exact logic I used when I was a Presbyterian minister to defend *sola Scriptura*.) Allow me to respond point by point:

1. **"Two points must be made concerning whether the Bible teaches *sola Scriptura*. First, as Catholic scholars themselves recognize, it is not necessary that the Bible explicitly and formally teach *sola Scriptura* in order for this doctrine to be true."**

Since no "Catholic scholar" of repute has ever taught *sola Scriptura* or said exactly what the authors claim, then they give an assumption that totally sidesteps the very question they are trying to prove. What does *sola Scriptura* mean except that the Bible *alone* is the one trustworthy foundation for what is true? If this is true, why shouldn't it necessarily be found in Scripture? Their argument begins by claiming that some un-named Catholic scholars (who do not believe in *sola Scriptura*) say that *sola Scriptura* doesn't have to be in Scripture. How does this prove anything? As in the logic of the commercial, the entire flow of the argument stalls where it starts.

2. "Many Christian teachings are a necessary logical deduction of what is clearly taught in the Bible (e.g., the Trinity)."

The authors believe they are providing evidence for their previous step, but it only shows their dependence upon the very assumption they are trying to prove. Belief in the Trinity is definitely *not* a "necessary logical deduction of what is clearly taught in the Bible" — as witnessed by the controversy over the doctrine in the early Church, and even in our own day (consider, e.g., Mormons and Jehovah's Witnesses). This, rather, is the presumption of *sola Scriptura* folk who have no other foundation upon which to base their belief in the Trinity.

The real foundation for Christian belief in the Trinity has more to do with the authority of Sacred Tradition. When the bishops of the Church gathered at the Council of Nicaea to discern what was the true Tradition as passed down from the churches of the Apostles, the scriptural witness was a portion of that Sacred Tradition. But the very heretics that the Council Fathers were fighting were the *sola Scriptura* representatives of their day. Based on the logic of their own interpretations, these heretics were proof-texting Scripture to propose a wide variety of heretical understandings of the relationship between God the Father, Jesus our Lord, and the Holy Spirit — precisely because the Trinity is *not* so "clearly taught in the Bible."

To describe the traditional teaching of the Trinity as a "necessary logical deduction" betrays a presupposition of *sola Scriptura* as the grid for interpreting the early Church. This is a form of circular logic, rather than examining the actual facts of doctrinal history.

3. "Likewise, it is possible that *sola Scriptura* could be a necessary logical deduction from what is taught in Scripture."

Since the logic of step two was flawed, then the "Likewise" of step three is unfounded. Interestingly, notice that the authors sheepishly refrain from claiming that *sola Scriptura* is a "necessary logical deduction from what is taught in Scripture." Rather, they said, "It is possible that [it] could be." Why so hesitant to make their case?

4. **"Second, the Bible does teach implicitly and logically, if not formally and explicitly, that the Bible alone is the only infallible basis for faith and practice. This it does in a number of ways."**

The authors now press forward, presuming they have sufficiently demonstrated that the belief that "the Bible *alone* is the only infallible basis for faith and practice" does not have to be "explicitly and formally taught" within this "only infallible" source of truth. Without suggesting an alternate authority for this belief, they quickly move to prove that the Bible does in fact teach this. I learned, from having lived for nearly forty years in the *sola Scriptura* camp, how dangerously easy it is to conclude almost anything "*implicitly and logically, if not formally and explicitly*" from Scripture. One can put together almost any three verses and make the Bible say whatever one wants it to say. Why is there a multitude of separate Christian traditions/denominations in the world, all teaching different theologies that they each believe are taught "*implicitly and logically, if not formally and explicitly*" in Scripture? Because the Bible *alone*, apart from Sacred Tradition and the teaching authority of the Church, was never intended to be the one "pillar and bulwark of the truth." Rather, Scripture says that this is the Church (see 1 Tim 3:15).

5. **"One, the fact that Scripture, without tradition, is said to be 'God-breathed' (*theopnuestos*) and thus by it believers are "competent, equipped for every good work" (2 Tim 3:16–17 NABRE) supports the doctrine of *sola Scriptura*."**

In essence, the authors are assuming as true the very thing they are trying to prove. Let me begin by actually quoting the Scripture passage they cite: "All Scripture is given by inspiration of God and is profitable for doctrine, for reproof, for correction, for instruction in righteousness, that the man of God may be complete, thoroughly equipped for every good work" (NKJV). Note first that the Apostle Paul does not say that only Scripture is "given by inspiration of God", or "God-breathed," let alone does he clarify what he means by "God-breathed." Nor does he say that the term "Scripture" that he uses is equivalent to what we mean two thousand years later by the term "Bible," a collection of books written over a thousand–year span by several dozen different authors, and which were not canonically defined until late in the fourth century by a group of Catholic bishops gathered in council. What Paul meant by "Scripture" he explains in the preceding verse, the "sacred writings" with which Timothy had "from childhood … been acquainted … which are able to instruct you for salvation through faith in Christ Jesus" (2 Tim 3:15, RSV2CE). This could only have been what we have come to call the Old Testament, since most, if not all, of the New Testament books had not been written when Timothy was a child, especially given that Paul was in the very process of writing one of them.

6. **"This flies in the face of the Catholic claim that the Bible is formally insufficient without the aid of tradition."**

To say that this argument consequently "flies in the face of the Catholic claim …" is quite a leap, because it is, essentially, an illogical conclusion from a previously insufficiently proven conclusion based upon a series of unproven assumptions. Once again, it rings of the illogical logic of the commercial.

7. **"St. Paul declares that the God-breathed writings are sufficient."**

Here the authors impose their own conclusions upon St. Paul. If St. Paul was implying that the books Timothy had known since childhood (i.e., the Old Testament) were sufficient (i.e., Old Testament *only*) "for salvation," then why was the New Testament needed, or why was the Ethiopian eunuch unable to understand the truth of the gospel from reading the Old Testament *alone* (Acts 8:27f.)? My argument here is hardly sufficient, of course, to address all the authors' assumptions, except to say that their proof-texting of inadequately defined terms does not necessarily "support the doctrine of *sola Scriptura*," as they claim in step five — unless one first presumes this doctrine and then interprets the Scriptures based upon this presumption.

Interestingly, these authors are of the theology that claims "good works" are no longer necessary, since we have been saved "by grace through faith" *alone*, yet the very verse they use to defend *sola Scriptura* states that the reason God inspired "all Scripture" was so that believers would be "competent, equipped for every good *work*." Ironically, here is another example of how a Protestant "tradition" can trump the clear teaching of Scripture.

8. **"And contrary to some Catholic apologists, limiting this to only the Old Testament will not help the Catholic cause for two reasons: first, the New Testament is also called "Scripture" (2 Pet 3:15–16; 1 Tim 5:18; cf. Lk 10:7); second, it is inconsistent to argue that God-breathed writings in the Old Testament are sufficient, but the inspired writings of the New Testament are not."**

First, the author's bold assertion that "the New Testament is also called 'Scripture,'" backed by their two proof-texts, is about as clearly proven as the last statement in the commercial's logic: "If you don't want to have a strange reputation with your cellmates, then you need to buy our product." The majority of all faithful Protestant and Catholic theologians do *not* make the extrapolation that what St. Peter said in 2 Peter 3:15–16 and what St. Paul said in 1 Timothy 5:18 proves that the entire New Testament is called "Scripture." It may be that St. Peter was viewing St. Paul's "letters" as somehow equivalent to "the rest of the Scriptures," but this involves reading a lot into this nebulous statement. What did St. Peter mean by "the rest of the Scriptures"? Since most Protestant and Catholic scholars agree that the early Church writers read and quoted from the Septuagint Greek version of the Old Testament, and since this included those "Apocryphal books" which Catholics include in the Bible but Protestants do not, does this imply that Sts. Peter and Paul also include these "Apocryphal books" in "the rest of Scripture"?

Second, the authors' second assertion is unfounded on several levels. First, no Catholic apologist or theologian has every claimed that either the Old or New Testament Scriptures are "sufficient." This has only been a Protestant claim since the Reformation, and this primarily by some who have insisted that the Greek term in this passage, ωφελιμοσ, means "sufficient" and not the normal meanings of "useful, beneficial, advantageous," as found in most translations.[13] Consequently, the charge that it would be "inconsistent to argue that God-breathed writings in the Old Testament are sufficient, but the inspired writings of the New Testament are not" is groundless and ineffectual. But this charge also begs the question — How did the New Testament writings come to be regarded as inspired in the first place? Who has the authority to determine and declare that the New Testament writings are inspired and equally as "useful, beneficial, advantageous" as the Old Testament Scriptures? Or which of the many books of antiquity are

---

13   Cf, William F. Arndt and F. Wilbur Gindrich, *A Greek-English Lexicon of the New Testament and other Early Christian Literature* (Chicago: University of Chicago Press, 1957), p. 909.

to be included in the inspired biblical collection? I believe the entire Bible is inspired and "useful" based upon the authority of the Church who, guided by the Holy Spirit, defined the canon of Scripture to include the New Testament books. *The canon of Scripture was not listed in any of the books themselves, but was essentially a part of Sacred Tradition.* The primary reason the statement might seem "inconsistent" is because there is no necessary direct connect between the inspiration of the Old Testament and/or the New Testament. We believe they are "inspired" because of the authority of the Church.

I trust that the authors of this article are good, faithful, Bible-believing, Christian brothers, and for that I rejoice and pray for their continual conversion in union with Christ. Unfortunately, however, their conclusions concerning *sola Scriptura* are based too much upon circular logic, beginning with the very assumption they are trying to prove. Why? Because, like the commercial, dare I say it: they want the people who trust in their authority to buy their product. Such is the danger of illogical logic.

5

THE PROBLEM WITH THE CANON[14]

REV. DWIGHT LONGENECKER

Pontius Pilate asked the basic question for all humanity when he asked Jesus, "What is Truth?" The irony of the scene is powerful and poignant because the incarnate Eternal Truth was standing before him. In John 14:6, Jesus proclaimed, "I am the way, the truth and the life." Elsewhere in the Gospel, Peter said, "Lord, to whom shall we go? You have the words of eternal life" (Jn 6:68). So the Christian answer to this profound question is that Jesus Himself is the Truth. If you want the truth, go to Him.

This is something upon which all Christians agree, but this answer does, however, raise more questions: How do we come to know Jesus as truth? How do we get in touch with this Jesus who is truth? We need answers to specific questions, like, what should we believe? How shall we behave? How shall we run the Church? Jesus may be the truth, but how do we get hold of that truth? How do we know that what we believe is His truth?

Most Evangelical Christians believe that the Bible is where we are to turn to learn what to believe and how to behave. This is because they believe that the Bible is inspired, or God-breathed, based upon St. Paul's words in 2 Timothy 3:16–17. However, since Paul wrote this text long before the idea of col-

---

14 This is a revised version of an article written by Rev. Dwight Longenecker originally titled "What Is Truth? An Examination of *Sola Scriptura*" that was part of his apologetics series for London's Premier Radio. Reprinted with permission.

lecting books into a "New Testament" even crossed anyone's mind, he could not have been referring to the New Testament. Paul — in writing to Timothy — could only have been talking about the Old Testament Scriptures.

The sad fact is that a striking majority of Christians know little about where the Bible came from and how it came to be. Far too many Christians act as if they believe that the Bible dropped down out of heaven in the King James Version.

Although nearly all Christians believe the Bible was inspired by God, this inspiration happened through real people in real situations in a real place and time. The Scriptures were written by the people of God, for the people of God. They were read by the people of God, used to teach the people of God, and used for the worship of the people of God. Maybe the best way to describe the Bible is to say that it is the story of the relationship between God and His people — the Church — both the Old Testament Church and the New Testament Church. The Bible was never just a list of things — a theological textbook — that God was telling His people they must believe. Neither was it merely a set of rules to be obeyed. Instead, the Bible was first and foremost the story of God's loving relationship with humanity.

Furthermore, the same people who wrote the Scriptures — used the Scriptures, prayed the Scriptures, and learned from the Scriptures — chose which holy writings should be included as Scripture. Before Christ was born, the books of what we now call the Old Testament were well established. During the first century of Christianity, the Gospels and Epistles were all written either by the Apostles chosen by Christ or one of their disciples. By the mid–second century, the early Christians were unanimous in accepting the four Gospels and the thirteen Letters of Paul. However, during these early centuries of the Church, many other writings appeared, vying for equal acceptance as apostolic documents. The question, in fact, was which books were to be read in the Sunday liturgies? Different local churches accepted varying and sometimes contradictory lists of books as authoritative, until finally in AD 382, at the Synod of Rome, a final canon of the books of the Old and New Testaments was presented. This is identical to the list found in any contemporary Catholic Bible.

This, therefore, draws our attention to another deep problem with *sola Scriptura*: Not only is the Bible itself impotent to prove its own inspiration or ensure its own interpretation, it does not specify exactly which of the hundreds of early Christian and pseudo-Christian writings were to be considered inspired Scripture. Was this a direct act of God, like Moses receiving the stone tablets? Or was the canon decided merely through a democratic vote of well-meaning, though now historically nameless, Christian leaders? If the latter were true, then why can't a different group of well-meaning Christian leaders gather and prayerfully decide on a new and different canon of Scripture? Actually, this was done during the Protestant Reformation, when seven of the Old Testament books included in the original fourth–century canon were removed as "Apocrypha." And if Luther had had his way, several New Testament books might also have been removed as "epistles of straw." Does just any well-meaning Christian have the authority to decide for himself which books are inspired, are to be included in the Bible, and how they are to be interpreted?

All of this raises the question: If God did provide His people with inspired writings, through His hand-chosen Apostles and their disciples, did He not also provide an inspired authority to ensure that the collection of writings was, indeed, the books His people were to read and prayerfully follow?

Some might argue that this was exactly what Jesus provided when He promised that He would send the Holy Spirit. In the

Gospel of John, we read that Jesus promised, "the Counselor, the Holy Spirit, whom the Father will send in my name, he will teach you all things, and bring to your remembrance all that I have said to you.... When the Spirit of truth comes, he will guide you into all the truth" (Jn 14:26; 16:13). Some might also point out that the Apostle John later reminded the Christians under his care that they had "been anointed by the Holy One," and therefore, all "know the truth," and "have no need that any one should teach [them]; as his anointing teaches [them] about everything" (1 Jn 2:20–27).

It is precisely because of this promise to His hand-chosen Apostles that we believe that the writings they left behind were "God-breathed" and that everything else Paul stated in 2 Timothy 3:16–17 is true. However, this still does not answer which of the hundreds of books were to be included in the New Testament, or even which of the many books were in fact written by an Apostle or his disciple. Many books not included in the New Testament make this claim. Nor do these promises of the Holy Spirit's anointing answer the problem of interpretation, for if John were to be taken literally, then, again, why so many conflicting interpretations? Is the Holy Spirit confused, or is it just us? And if it's us, then how can anyone be sure that his or her interpretation is reliable? And finally, if the gift of the Holy Spirit to each Christian was to ensure the trustworthiness of private interpretation, with no further need for teachers, then why did John have to write this? Wouldn't they already know it through their anointing? In fact, if the indwelling of the Holy Spirit leads all Christians into truth, then why is there a New Testament at all? Does not the existence of the New Testament Gospels and Letters prove, rather, that Spirit-filled Christians still need authoritative Spirit-filled leaders to help them interpret how to understand and apply the truth of the Gospel to their lives? Even to know precisely what the gospel is?

Jesus said, "If you continue in my word, you are truly my disciples, and you will know the truth, and the truth will make you free" (Jn 8:31–32). Is the Bible equivalent to His Word? Is His Word limited to the words contained in the Bible? Can you determine from the Bible *alone* the truth and meaning of His Word, so that you can be certain that you are truly His disciple? Are you free? Are you certain that your interpretation of the Bible is eternally true, when, no matter what interpretation you hold, there are at least dozens of contradicting opinions held by equally certain Christians for the same texts of Scripture — who believe differently about what is necessary to be saved?

We are brought all the way back to where we began: "What is truth?" How can you or I be certain that our grasp of truth is any more certain than that of Pontius Pilate?

REV. DWIGHT LONGENECKER *is a former Anglican priest who was received into the Catholic Church along with his family in 1995. He was ordained as a Catholic priest for the Diocese of Charleston, South Carolina, in December of 2006. Rev. Longenecker is an author, a blogger, and the editor of a best-selling book of English conversion stories called* The Path to Rome: Modern Journeys to the Catholic Faith *(Gracewing, 2010). Read Fr. Longenecker's popular blog, browse his books, and be in touch at dwightlongenecker.com.*

6

MORE ILLOGIC CONCERNING *SOLA SCRIPTURA*[15]

REV. BRIAN W. HARRISON

As an active Protestant in my mid–twenties, I began to feel that I might have a vocation to become a minister. The trouble was that while I had quite definite convictions about the things that most Christians have traditionally held in common — the sort of thing C.S. Lewis termed "mere Christianity" — I had had some firsthand experience with several denominations (Presbyterian, Anglican, Lutheran, Methodist) and was far from certain as to which of them (if any) had an overall advantage over the others. So I began to think, study, search, and pray. Was there a true Church? If so, how was one to decide which? The more I studied, the more perplexed I became.

At one point my elder sister, a very committed Evangelical with somewhat flexible denominational affiliations, chided me with becoming "obsessed" with trying to find a "true Church." "Does it really matter?" she would ask. Well, yes it did. It was all very well for a lay Protestant to relegate the denominational issue to a fairly low priority amongst religious questions: lay people can go to one Protestant church one week and another

---

15 This is a revised version of an article written by Rev. Brian W. Harrison originally titled "Logic and the Foundations of Protestantism." The original article first appeared in the Fall 1990 issue of FAITH & REASON published by Christendom College Press. Reprinted with permission.

the next week, and nobody really worries too much. But an ordained minister obviously cannot do that. He must make a serious commitment to a definite church community, and under normal circumstances that commitment will be expected to last a lifetime. So clearly that choice had to be made with a deep sense of responsibility; and the time to make it was before, not after, ordination.

As matters turned out, my search lasted several years, and eventually led me to where I never suspected it would at first. I shall not attempt to relate the full story, but will focus on just one aspect of the question as it developed for me — an aspect that seems quite fundamental.

As I groped and prayed my way towards a decision — contemplating the mountains of erudition, the vast labyrinth of conflicting interpretations of Christianity (not to mention other faiths) that lined the shelves of religious bookshops and libraries — I at times came close to despair and agnosticism. If all the "experts" on truth — the great theologians, historians, philosophers — disagreed interminably with each other, then how did God, if He was really there, expect me, an ordinary "Joe Blow," to work out what was true?

The more I became enmeshed in specific questions of biblical interpretation — of who had the right understanding of justification, of the Eucharist, Baptism, grace, Christology, church government and discipline, and so on — the more I came to feel that this whole line of approach was a hopeless quest, a blind alley. These were all questions that required a great deal of erudition, learning, competence in biblical exegesis, patristics, history, metaphysics, ancient languages — in short, scholarly research. But was it really credible (I began to ask myself) that God, if He were to reveal the truth about these disputed questions at all, would make this truth so inaccessible that only a small scholarly elite had even the faintest chance of reaching it? Wasn't that a kind of gnosticism? Where did it leave the non-scholarly bulk of the human race? It didn't seem to make sense. If, as they say, war is too important to be left to the generals, then revealed truth seemed too important to be left to the biblical scholars. It was no use saying that perhaps God simply expected the non-scholars to trust the scholars. How were they to know which scholars to trust, given that the scholars all contradicted each other?

Therefore, in my efforts to break out of the dense exegetical undergrowth where I could not see the trees for the wood, I shifted towards a new emphasis in my truth-seeking criteria: I tried to get beyond the bewildering mass of contingent historical and linguistic data upon which the rival exegetes and theologians constructed their doctrinal castles, in order to concentrate on those elemental, necessary principles of human thought which are accessible to all of us, learned and unlearned alike. In a word, I began to suspect that an emphasis on logic, rather than on research, might expedite an answer to my prayers for guidance.

The advantage was that you don't need to be learned to be logical. You need not have spent years amassing mountains of information in libraries in order to apply the first principles of reason. You can apply them from the comfort of your armchair, so to speak, in order to test the claims of any body of doctrine, on any subject whatsoever, that comes claiming your acceptance. Moreover logic, like mathematics, yields firm certitude, not mere changeable opinions and provisional hypotheses. Logic is the first natural "beacon of light" with which God has provided us as intelligent beings living in a world darkened by the confusion of countless conflicting attitudes, doctrines, and worldviews, all telling us how to live our lives during this brief time that is given to us here on earth.

Logic of course has its limits. Pure "armchair" reasoning alone will never be able to tell you the meaning of your life and how you should live it. But as far as it goes, logic is an indispensable tool, and I even suspect that you sin against God, the first truth, if you knowingly flout or ignore it in your thinking. "Thou shalt not contradict thyself" seems to me an important precept of the natural moral law.

Be that as it may, I found that the main use of logic, in my quest for religious truth, turned out to be in deciding not what was true, but what was false. If someone presents you with a system of ideas or doctrines that logical analysis reveals to be coherent — that is, free from internal contradictions and meaningless absurdities — then you can conclude, "This set of ideas may be true. It has at least passed the first test of truth — the coherence test." To find out if it actually is true, you will then have to leave your logician's armchair and seek further information. But if it fails this most elementary test of truth, it can safely be eliminated without further ado from the ideological competition, no matter how many impressive-looking volumes of erudition may have been written in support of it, and no matter how attractive and appealing many of its features (or many of its proponents) may appear.

Some readers may wonder why I am laboring the point about logic. Isn't all this perfectly obvious? Well, it ought to be obvious to everyone, and is indeed obvious to many, including those who have had the good fortune of receiving a classical Catholic education. Catholicism, as I came to discover, has a quite positive approach to our natural reasoning powers, and traditionally has its future priests study philosophy for years before they even begin theology. But I came from a religious milieu where this outlook was not encouraged — indeed, was often even discouraged. The Protestant Reformers taught that original sin has so weakened the human intellect that we must be extremely cautious about the claims of "proud reason." Luther called reason the "devil's whore" — a siren which seduced men into grievous error. "Don't trust your reason, just bow humbly before God's truth revealed to you in His holy Word, the Bible!" — this was pretty much the message that came through to me from the Calvinist and Lutheran circles that influenced me most in the first few years after I made my "decision for Christ" at the age of 18. The Reformers themselves were forced to employ reason even while denouncing it, in their efforts to rebut the biblical arguments of their "papist" foes. And that, it seemed to me, was rather illogical on their part.

LOGIC AND THE *SOLA SCRIPTURA* PRINCIPLE

Thus, with my awakening interest in logical analysis as a test of religious truth, I was naturally led to ask whether this illogicality in the practice of the Reformers was, perhaps, accompanied by illogicality at the more fundamental level of their theory. As a good Protestant, I had been brought up to hold as sacred the basic methodological principle of the Reformation: that the Bible alone contains all the truth that God has revealed for our salvation. Churches that held to that principle were at least "respectable," one was given to understand, even though they might differ considerably from each other in regard to the interpretation of Scripture. But as for Roman Catholicism and other churches that unashamedly added their own traditions to the Word of God — were they not self-evidently outside the pale? Were they not condemned out of their own mouths?

But when I got down to making a serious attempt to explore the implications of this rock-bottom dogma of the Reformers, I could not avoid the conclusion that it was rationally indefensible. This is demonstrated in the following eight steps, which embody nothing more than simple, common-sense logic, and a couple of indisputable, empirically observable facts about the Bible:

1. The Reformers asserted Proposition A: "All revealed truth is to be found in the inspired Scriptures." However, this is quite useless unless we know which books are meant by the "inspired Scriptures." After all, many different sects and religions have many different books, which they call "inspired Scriptures."

2. The theory we are considering, when it talks of "inspired Scriptures," means in fact those 66 books, which are bound and published in Protestant Bibles. For convenience, we shall refer to them from now on simply as "the 66 books."

3. The precise statement of the theory we are examining thus becomes Proposition B: "All revealed truth is to be found in the 66 books."

4. It is a fact that nowhere in the 66 books themselves can we find any statements telling us which books make up the entire corpus of inspired Scripture. There is no complete list of inspired books anywhere within their own pages, nor can such a list be compiled by putting isolated verses together. (This would be the case: [a] if you could find verses like "Esther is the Word of God," "This Gospel is inspired by God," "The Second Letter of Peter is inspired Scripture," etc., for all of the 66 books; and [b] if you could also find a biblical passage stating that no books other than these 66 were to be held as inspired. Obviously, nobody could even pretend to find all this information about the canon of Scripture in the Bible itself.)

5. It follows that Proposition B — the very foundation of all Protestant Christianity — is neither found in Scripture nor can it be deduced from Scripture in any way. Since the 66 books are not even identified in Scripture, much less can

any further information about them (e.g., that all revealed truth is contained in them) be found there. In short, we must affirm Proposition C: "Proposition B is an addition to the 66 books."

6. It follows immediately from the truth of Proposition C that Proposition B cannot itself be revealed truth. To assert that it is would involve a self-contradictory statement: "All revealed truth is to be found in the 66 books, but this revealed truth itself is not found there."

7. Could it be the case that Proposition B is true, but is not revealed truth? If that is the case, then it must be either something which can be deduced from revealed truth or something which natural human reason alone can discover, without any help from revelation. The first possibility is ruled out because, as we saw in steps 4 and 5, B cannot be deduced from Scripture, and to postulate some other revealed extra-scriptural premise from which B might be deduced would contradict B itself. The second possibility involves no self-contradiction, but it is factually preposterous, and I doubt whether any Protestant has seriously tried to defend it — least of all those traditional Protestants who strongly emphasize the corruption of man's natural intellectual powers as a result of the Fall.

Human reason might well be able to conclude prudently and responsibly that an authority which itself claimed to possess the totality of revealed truth was in fact justified in making that claim, provided that this authority backed up the claim by some very striking evidence. (Catholics, in fact, believe that their Church is precisely such an authority.) But how could reason alone reach that same well-founded certitude about a collection of 66 books which do not even lay claim to what is attributed to them? (The point is reinforced when we remember that those who attribute the totality of revealed truth to the 66 books, namely Protestant church members, are very ready to acknowledge their own fallibility — whether individually or collectively — in matters of religious doctrine. All Protestant churches deny their own infallibility as much as they deny the Pope's.)

8. Since Proposition B is not revealed truth, nor a truth which can be deduced from revelation, nor a naturally knowable truth, it is not true at all. Therefore, the basic doctrine for which the Reformers fought is simply false.

CALVIN'S ATTEMPTED SOLUTION

How did the Reformers try to cope with this fundamental weakness in the logical structure of their own first principles? John Calvin, usually credited with being the most systematic and coherent thinker of the Reformation, tried to justify belief in the divine authorship of the 66 books by dogmatically postulating a direct communication of this knowledge from God to the individual believer. Calvin makes it clear that in saying Scripture is "self-authenticated," he does not mean to be taken literally and absolutely. He does not mean that some Bible text or other affirms that the 66 books, and they alone, are divinely inspired. As we observed in step 4 above, nobody ever could claim anything so patently false. Calvin simply means that no extra-biblical human testimony, such as that of Church tradition, is needed in order for individuals to know that these books are inspired. We can summarize his view as Proposition D: "The Holy Spirit teaches Christians individually, by a direct inward testimony, that the 66 books are inspired by God."

The trouble is that the Holy Spirit Himself is an extra-biblical authority as much as a pope or council. The third Person of the Trinity is clearly not identical with the truths He has expressed, through human authors, in the Bible. It follows that even if Calvin's Proposition D is true, it contradicts Proposition

B, for "if all revealed truth is to be found in the 66 books," then that leaves no room for the Holy Spirit to reveal directly and nonverbally one truth which cannot be found in any passage of those books, namely, the fact that each one of them is inspired.

In any case, even if Calvin could somehow show that D did not itself contradict B, he would still not have succeeded in showing that B is true. Even if we were to accept the extremely implausible view represented by Proposition D, that would not prove that no other writings are inspired; much less would it prove that there are no revealed truths that come to us through tradition rather than through inspired writings. In short, Calvin's defense of biblical inspiration in no way overthrows our eight–step disproof of the *sola Scriptura* principle. Indeed, it does not even attempt to establish that principle as a whole, but only one aspect of it — that is, which books are to be understood by the term "*Scriptura.*"

The schizoid history of Protestantism itself bears witness to the original inner contradiction which marked its conception and birth. Conservative Protestants have maintained the original insistence on the Bible as the unique infallible source of revealed truth, at the price of logical incoherence. Liberals on the other hand have escaped the incoherence while maintaining the claim to "private interpretation" over against that of popes and councils, but at the price of abandoning the Reformers' insistence on an infallible Bible. They thereby effectively replace revealed truth by human opinion, and faith by an autonomous reason. Thus, in the liberal/Evangelical split within Protestantism since the eighteenth century, we see both sides teaching radically opposed doctrines, even while each claims to be the authentic heir of the Reformation. The irony is that both sides are right: their conflicting beliefs are simply the two horns of a dilemma that has been tearing at the inner fabric of Protestantism ever since its turbulent beginnings.

Reflections such as these from a Catholic onlooker may seem a little hard or unyielding to some — ill-suited, perhaps, to a climate of ecumenical dialogue in which gentle suggestion, rather than blunt affirmation, is the preferred mode of discourse. But logic is of its very nature hard and unyielding; and insofar as truth and honesty are to be the hallmarks of true ecumenism, the claims of logic will have to be squarely faced, not politely avoided.

REV. BRIAN W. HARRISON *is a convert to the Catholic Church and was ordained a priest in 1985. He is a priest of the Society of the Oblates of Wisdom and a retired professor of theology at the Pontifical University of Puerto Rico, Ponce.*

7

ORAL TRADITION AND THE NEW TESTAMENT[16]

DAVID PALM

The Church did not pass on the teachings of Christ only in written form. From the earliest days, the teaching was also passed on through the preaching and teaching of the Apostles and their disciples. In his letters to the young bishop Timothy, Paul wrote, "Attend to the public reading of Scripture, to preaching, to teaching," and "continue in what you have learned … knowing from whom you learned it and how from childhood you have been acquainted with the Sacred Writings" (1 Tim 4:13; 2 Tim 3:14–15).

Of course, in these passages, Paul could only have been referring to the Old Testament, which he therefore held as authoritative. But he also believed that his own teaching, both written and preached, was to be taken as authoritative for determining doctrine and right Christian behavior. This is stated most clearly in Paul's Second Letter to the Thessalonians: "So then brothers, stand firm and hold to the traditions which you were taught by us, either by word of mouth or by letter" (2:15). So the teachings that Paul received from Jesus he passed on both in writing and by word of mouth.

16 This is a revised version of an article by David Palm originally titled "Oral Tradition in the New Testament," (*This Rock* magazine, May 1995; reprint, http://www.ewtn.com/library/ANSWERS/ORALTRAD.HTM), with some additions from an article titled "What Is Truth? An Examination of *Sola Scriptura*," by Rev. Dwight Longenecker that was part of his apologetics series for London's Premier Radio. Reprinted with permission.

There are many who believe that oral Tradition lost its authority as soon as the biblical books were written down, but it is significant to recognize that in the very quote above, Paul acknowledges that both sources of teaching existed side by side when he wrote to the Thessalonians. We also see that while Paul was writing what would later be declared inspired Scripture, he was not only receiving oral Tradition from others, but continuing to pass it on to his hearers: "By [the gospel I preached to you] ... you are saved if you hold it fast ... For I delivered to you as of first importance what I also received." (1 Cor 15:2–3).

Paul promotes the continuing importance of oral teaching as well as written when he tells Timothy: "Follow the pattern of sound words which you have heard from me, in the faith and love which are in Christ Jesus; guard the truth that has been entrusted to you" (2 Tim 1:13). Elsewhere he praises the Corinthians for "maintain[ing] the traditions even as I have delivered them to you" (1 Cor 11:2).

Did Paul think this oral teaching was to be passed on? Paul said to Timothy, "What you have heard from me before many witnesses entrust to faithful men who will be able to teach others also" (2 Tim 2:2). In other words, he commanded Timothy to hand on the oral Tradition that he had received from Paul. It's interesting that in this passage Paul is referring to four generations of succession — his own, Timothy's, the people Timothy would teach, and the ones they in turn would teach — which the Church would later identify as the process of apostolic succession.

The documents of the early Church in the years just after the death of the Apostles show that they believed their Church leaders had indeed inherited a precious deposit of faith — both in the writings of the Apostles and in the oral traditions of the Apostles. As a writer about AD 160 explains, "The faith of the Gospels is established, and the Tradition of the Apostles is preserved."[17]

Writing about the year AD 189, Irenaeus, bishop of Lyons, wrote: "What if the Apostles had not left writings to us? Would it not be necessary to follow the order of tradition which was handed down to those to whom they entrusted the churches?"[18] Elsewhere Irenaeus also pointed out how important this Apostolic Tradition was for people to know the full truth: "It is possible then for everyone in every church who may wish to know the truth to contemplate the Traditions of the Apostles which has been made known throughout the whole world."[19]

This helps us answer the difficult question: Where do we turn for a faithful interpretation of the Bible? Is there a body of teaching that has been faithfully passed down from the Apostles that would help us to interpret the Scriptures the right way? If such a body of teaching exists, then it provides a rich mine for us to turn to when we try to interpret Scripture. If an ancient strand of teaching exists, which goes back to the Apostles themselves, then we have not only the Scriptures for a source book, but we have a rich tapestry of teaching which helps us to understand the Scriptures.

So when we have a difficult question of biblical interpretation, we don't just read the rest of the Bible to find the answer. We turn to the Tradition as preserved and protected by the Church to see what the people of God believed before us. Did they face the same questions? How did they answer them? Did they face similar circumstances? How did they confront them? Did they face the same doubts, problems, heresies, and attacks? How did they stand up for the truth in their day? How can it help us determine the truth today?

17 *To Diognetus* 11, as quoted in *The Fathers Know Best* by Jimmy Akin (San Diego: Catholic Answers, 2010), p. 167.

18 *Against Heresies*, 3,2:1.

19 *Against Heresies*, 3,3:1.

Throughout the New Testament, the apostolic authors draw on the Old Testament Scriptures as the foundations for what they believe. Herein lies one of the arguments used to defend *sola Scriptura*. But is there any evidence that any New Testament author cited Hebrew oral Tradition as authoritative for doctrine? Surprisingly, at least to some, there are several instances where oral Tradition is cited in the Bible to support Christian doctrine.

We can divide these examples into two categories.

First, we find passages in the New Testament in which oral Tradition is cited in support of doctrine. This evidence is particularly significant because it shows that, for the Apostles, oral Tradition was trustworthy when formulating and developing elements of the Christian Faith. This becomes an excellent biblical precedent for the Church's historical practice of basing some Christian dogmas primarily on Tradition rather than on explicit biblical testimony.

In a second category of passages, the New Testament authors draw on oral Tradition, but not so explicitly in support of doctrine. These examples are significant in that they show the extent to which the earliest Christians, including the Apostles themselves, reckoned with the twin witnesses of Scripture and Tradition when they expounded the faith.

DOCTRINAL EXAMPLES

MATTHEW 2:23

Scripture says that Joseph and Mary returned to Nazareth after their sojourn in Egypt, "that what was spoken by the prophets might be fulfilled, 'He shall be called a Nazarene'" (Mt 2:23). All commentators admit that the phrase "He shall be called a Nazarene" is not found anywhere in the Old Testament. Yet Matthew tells us that the Holy Family fulfilled this prophecy, which had been passed on "by the prophets."

The proposed solutions to explain this verse are legion. They range from trying to find some wordplay on "Nazarene" in the Hebrew text of the Old Testament, to viewing this text as loosely "fulfilling" a conglomeration of Old Testament passages that refer to a despised Messiah. The serious grappling by scholars with the text is admirable, but in the end their solutions seem farfetched.

It may be that we should seek resolution in simplicity. When read in Greek, the introduction to this prophecy differs from all the other "fulfillment" sayings in Matthew (for example, Mt 1:22, 2:15, 3:15, and others). Thus, the failed attempts to locate the Old Testament background to this prophecy, coupled with this unique introduction, suggest that the simplest solution is probably the correct one: Matthew is drawing on oral Tradition for this saying. If this is the case, it is significant that he places this prophecy on the same level as ones he attributes to specific authors of the Old Testament. This then would be an example of God's own Word being passed on via oral Tradition and not through written Scripture.

MATTHEW 23:2

Just before launching into a blistering denunciation of the scribes and Pharisees, Jesus delivers this command to the crowds: "The scribes and Pharisees sit on Moses' seat; so practice and observe whatever they tell you, but not what they do; for they preach, but do not practice" (Mt 23:2–3).

Although Jesus strongly indicts His opponents of hypocrisy for not following their own teaching, He nevertheless insists that the scribes and Pharisees hold a position of legitimate authority, which He characterizes as sitting "on Moses' seat." One searches in vain for any reference to this seat of Moses in the Old Testament. But it was commonly understood in ancient Israel that there was an authoritative teaching office, passed on by Moses to his successors.

As the first verse of the tractate Abôte in the Mishna (a collection of Jewish oral Tradition) indicates, the Jews understood that God's revelation, received by Moses, had been handed down from him in uninterrupted succession, through Joshua, the elders, the prophets, and the great Sanhedrin (Acts 15:21). The scribes and Pharisees participated in this authoritative line, and as such their teaching deserved to be respected.

Jesus here draws on oral Tradition to uphold the legitimacy of this teaching office in Israel. In upholding the legitimacy of both Scripture and Tradition, the Church in her teaching office, therefore, follows the example of Jesus Himself.

In addition, we see that the structure of the Church — with an authoritative teaching office comprised of bishops who are the direct successors of the Apostles — follows the example of ancient Israel. While there are groups of Christians today that deny continuity between Israel and the Church, historic orthodox Christianity has always understood the Church to be a fulfillment of Israel. This verse about Moses' chair illuminates why whenever the successor of Peter gives a solemn teaching for the whole Church, he is said to speak *ex cathedra* or "from the chair."

Whereas under the Old Covenant the administration of God's people came from the "chair of Moses," Christians under the New Covenant look to the "chair of Peter" for direction on questions of faith and morals. But there is a notable difference between the teaching authority under the Old Covenant and the Magisterium under the New Covenant. The successors of the Apostles, and especially Peter's successor, have the Holy Spirit to guide them into all truth, and they have Jesus' promise that the gates of hell will not prevail against the Church (Mt 16:17–19).

1 CORINTHIANS 10:4

Paul shows how Christian sacraments — Baptism and the Eucharist — were prefigured in the Old Testament. He treats Baptism first: "Our fathers were all under the cloud, and all passed through the sea, and all were baptized into Moses in the cloud and in the sea" (1 Cor 10:1-2). Next he highlights the Eucharist, prefigured by the manna in the wilderness (v. 3; cf. Jn 6:26-40), and the water that God provided for Israel: "All drank the same supernatural drink. For they drank from the supernatural Rock which followed them, and the Rock was Christ" (1 Cor 10:4).

The Old Testament says nothing about any movement of the rock that Moses struck to provide water for the Israelites (Ex 17:1-7, Num 20:2-13), but in rabbinic Tradition, the rock actually followed them on their journey through the wilderness. In a further development, another Tradition, given by Philo, even equates this rock with preexistent Wisdom: "For the flinty rock is the Wisdom of God, which he marked off highest and chiefest from his powers, and from which he satisfies the thirsty souls that love God."[20]

It seems that Paul is drawing on this Tradition, but he elevates it to an even higher level. Christ Himself was the Rock who provided for the people of Israel, which in turn makes their rebellion all the more heinous (1 Cor 10:5ff.). Paul does not hesitate to draw on stock oral Tradition to illustrate and enhance his presentation of the gospel. The details provided in these Traditions preserved under the Old Covenant shed fresh light on the preparation that God made through Israel for the building of His Church and on the characteristics of the Christian sacraments.

....
20   *Allegorical Interpretation of Genesis* 2,3, 2.86.

JUDE 9

Jude relates an altercation between Michael and Satan: "When the archangel Michael, contending with the devil, disputed about the body of Moses, he did not presume to pronounce a reviling judgment upon him, but said, 'The Lord rebuke you'" (Jude 9).

Nowhere else in Scripture is there mention of this incident. Jude writes, however, as if it is already well-known to his readers. Some versions of the story circulating in ancient Judaism depict Satan trying to intervene as Michael buries the body. Several of the Church Fathers know of another version in which Moses' body is assumed into heaven after his death. Jude draws on this oral Tradition to highlight the incredible arrogance of the heretics he opposes; even Michael the archangel did not take it upon himself to rebuke Satan, and yet these men have no scruples in reviling celestial beings. This text provides another example of a New Testament author tapping oral Tradition to expound Christian doctrine — in this case, an issue of behavior.

JUDE 14–15

This one's a real showstopper, perhaps the best example of all. St. Jude speaks of the rebellious upstarts of his day, saying, "It was of these also that Enoch in the seventh generation from Adam prophesied, saying, 'Behold, the Lord came with myriads of his holy ones, to execute judgment on all, and to convict all the ungodly of all their deeds of ungodliness which they have committed in such an ungodly way, and of all the harsh things which ungodly sinners have spoken against him.'"

This statement may also be found in the non-scriptural book of 1 Enoch (1:9), but Jude's use of it does not really say anything about the inspiration of 1 Enoch. Rather, he asserts that the saying itself actually hales from the venerable Enoch, whose righteous life is mentioned in Genesis 5.

Here is a tradition, a prophetic revelation, which was passed on orally for *millennia* before being captured first in a non-inspired written document (1 Enoch) and then in an inspired document (Jude). Did the writers of the New Testament ever regard oral Tradition as divine revelation? This example more than any other shows that the answer to that is a resounding, Yes!

OTHER EXAMPLES

There are a number of other examples in the New Testament in which the writer likely draws on oral tradition, but not so clearly in support of any doctrine. For instance, Paul dips into rabbinic tradition to supply the names, Jannes and Jambres, of the magicians who opposed Moses in Pharaoh's court (2 Tim 3:8). In the Old Testament, these individuals are anonymous (Ex 7:8ff.). James tells us that because of Elijah's prayer there was no rain in Israel for three years (Jas 5:17), but the Old Testament account of Elijah's altercation with King Ahab says nothing of him praying for a drought (1 Kgs 17). It is rabbinic tradition that characterizes Elijah as the quintessential man of prayer. And even the Golden Rule, "So whatever you wish that men would do to you, do so to them; for this is the law and the prophets" (Mt 7:12) was anticipated by Jewish oral Tradition. Rabbi Hillel taught, "What you do not like should be done to you, do not to your fellow; this is the whole Torah, all the rest is commentary."[21]

CONCLUSION

Likely there are many more examples of the use of oral Tradition in the New Testament. Reference works such as Alfred Edersheim's *The Life and Times of Jesus the Messiah*, John Lightfoot's *Commentary on the New Testament from the*

---

21 Babylonian Talmud, *Shabbat 31a.*

Talmud and Hebraica, and Strack and Billerbeck's magisterial *Kommentar zum Neuen Testament aus Talmud und Misrasch* contain a wealth of parallels between rabbinic tradition and the New Testament writings. One notoriously difficult impediment to such a study is determining which traditions predate the New Testament and which are exclusively post-apostolic; such decisions must be left to experts. Nevertheless, these passages strongly suggest that the New Testament authors drew on oral Tradition as they expounded the Christian Faith. This fact spells real trouble for any Christian who asserts that we must find all of our doctrines in written Scripture. The Apostles did not teach the doctrine of *sola Scriptura* explicitly in Scripture, and, through their use of oral Tradition, they did not intend to teach it implicitly by their example either. The conclusion is that they simply did not hold to a principle of *sola Scriptura.*

DAVID PALM, *a convert to Catholicism, is a husband and father of four. He holds an M.A. in New Testament Studies from Trinity Evangelical Divinity School and works professionally as an electrical engineer.*

8

WHEN TRADITION IS TREATED LIKE REVELATION[22]

MARK P. SHEA

Do Bible-only Christians ever treat extra-biblical Tradition as authoritative revelation? In other words, is it really the case that all Evangelical belief is derived from the clear and unambiguous teaching of the Bible alone? Do Bible-only Christians really speak forth only what Scripture speaks, keep silent where Scripture is silent, and never bind the conscience of the believer on those questions in which Scripture permits different interpretations? More specifically, is there any evidence of Tradition being treated like revelation? Are there any rock-bottom, non-negotiable, can't-do-without-'em beliefs that are not attested (or only very weakly attested) in the Bible, yet which orthodox Evangelicals treat like revelation? If such things are found, and if they have an ancient pedigree, this would seem to be very strong evidence that the Apostolic Tradition not only was larger than the Bible alone, but had — somehow — been handed down to the present.

Consider, for example, the following nonnegotiables.

---

22 This chapter is a revised version of an article written by Mark P. Shea originally titled "When Evangelicals Treat Catholic Tradition Like Revelation," which appeared in the September 1996 issue of the *New Oxford Review*, which itself was an adaptation from his book, *By What Authority?: An Evangelical Discovers Catholic Tradition* (Huntington: Our Sunday Visitor Books, 1996). Reprinted with permission.

THE SANCTITY OF HUMAN LIFE

Arguably the most pressing issue of our time is the question of the sanctity of human life from conception to natural death. While you are reading this, several thousand preborn babies, ranging in age from first trimester to full term, are going to be legally suctioned, burned, dismembered, or decapitated by skilled professionals. As this evil occurs, a bewildered modern society, long ago cut adrift from its Christian roots, will not recoil in horror but will instead flop its hands passively in its lap, register a befuddled shrug of discomfort, and continue lacking the capacity to tell whether or not this is bad.

Meanwhile, the culture of death will not sleep. Rather, emboldened by our moral paralysis in the face of so obvious an evil, the purveyors of "choice" will ask ever more loudly, "If we can do these things when the tree is green, what can we get away with when it is dry? If the life of the helpless infant is cheap when the economy is strong, why not the life of the disabled, aged, and sick when medical costs skyrocket?"

For many, the question of the sanctity of human life is a bedrock of Christian morals. If the protection of life from conception to natural death isn't essential to Christian teaching, what is? Surely, here we ought to find a sharp dichotomy between the Church and the modern world. Right?

Wrong. The plain fact is, things don't break down that way. On one side of the cultural divide are not only secularists, but, alas, many Christians who, with trembling devotion to the spirit of the age, dutifully parrot the rhetoric that those who defend human life are "antichoice."

On the other side of the divide are most Evangelicals, conservative members of the mainline Protestant churches, the Catholic and Orthodox Churches, and conservative Jews.

Yet for twenty centuries, absolutely all of Christianity stood staunchly behind the defenseless ones against the culture of death. Indeed, so recent is the minting of the "right to choose" that not even theological liberals were willing to call abortion anything other than a grave sin until the past few decades. That is why we can scarcely find a shred of Christian theology written in favor of abortion and euthanasia before the 1960s and '70s. From the first century to the present, a shoreless ocean of testimony from every sector of the Church decries this terrible crime against God and humanity. And Evangelicals, with very few exceptions, are of one voice with twenty centuries of Christian preaching concerning this most elementary of Christian moral truths. However, is the irrefutable basis for pro-life convictions Scripture *alone*?

There are many scriptural foundations for pro-life convictions: "For you formed my inward being; you knitted me together in my mother's womb" (Ps 139:13), "Before I formed you in the womb I knew you" (Jer 1:5), and so forth. These verses bear oblique witness to a pro-life position, and it is undeniable that the pro-life position is an obvious fact of Christian teaching throughout all ages. But it is next to impossible from Scripture *alone* to argue against abortion and for a devotion to the sanctity of preborn life as an intrinsic, absolutely essential, utterly nonnegotiable part of the Christian Faith. For the fact is, a modern apologist for the culture of death can and does argue that Scripture alone, apart from Tradition, is as ambiguous about abortion as it is about the question of just war vs. pacifism — and therefore abortion is a matter of "Christian liberty."

Consider: Neither Testament gives a clear understanding of the status of unborn life. Is the fetus a human person possessing the same dignity as an infant after birth? Is the conceptus? Is the act of directly causing the death of such a one an act of murder or some lesser offense? Is it an offense at all? No direct answer is ever attempted to these questions anywhere in Scripture.

Worse, the indirect ways in which Scripture addresses these issues are very oblique and open to multiple interpretations — apart from Tradition. Thus Exodus 21:22 reads: "When men strive together, and hurt a woman with child, so that there is a miscarriage, and yet no harm follows, the one who hurt her shall be fined, according as the woman's husband shall lay upon him; and he shall pay as the judges determine. If any harm follows, then you shall give life for life, eye for eye, tooth for tooth, hand for hand, foot for foot, burn for burn, wound for wound, stripe for stripe."

Far more questions are raised by this passage than are answered — if we are left to interpret it without reference to Jewish and Christian Tradition, as pro-choice Christians urge us to do. For instance, the Hebrew word which is here translated "there is a miscarriage" is in fact much more flexible than this. It means "departs" and can be read as "gives birth prematurely" or as "spontaneously aborts." So, does the caveat about "harm" apply to the woman or to the miscarried child? Does the Law demand wound for wound for the harm done to the mother or the unborn? If the mother is not seriously injured but the child dies, is this what is meant by "no harm"? The text does not say. Nor does the rest of Scripture help us.

Similarly, the New Testament does not tell us how to understand another difficult Old Testament passage: Numbers 5:20–27. This strange text prescribes an ordeal for suspected adulteresses, in which the suspected woman is placed under oath and made to drink "water of bitterness." The purpose of the ordeal was to call down a divine curse on the adulteress that would cause her "body to swell and [her] thigh to fall away" or as the footnotes to the NIV Bible put it, to make her "be barren and have a miscarrying womb."

If we do not have a larger Tradition for understanding such a text — if we "let Scripture interpret Scripture" as most

Evangelicals say — it seems that *some* induced miscarriages (i.e., those of adulteresses) ought to be countenanced by the people of God. In short, Scripture does not automatically give one the impression that the Bible lends itself to an irrefutable case for the sanctity of every human life from conception to natural death.

At this, some Evangelicals may attempt to create a larger interpretive context by "letting Scripture interpret Scripture" again. They might raise the counterexample of John the Baptist, moved by the Spirit in Elizabeth's womb when Mary arrived (Lk 1:41). Is not this a strong indication that even unborn children are persons responsive to the Spirit of God? Is it not a pretty good hint that unborn babies are people too?

Of course it is. That is, it's a "strong indication" — a hint, a sign, a good possibility. It is not, however, incontrovertible *proof* that all children are similarly graced with supernatural gifts, including the supernatural gift of personhood, when they are as yet unformed in their mother's womb. Unfortunately, there are Christians who have actually taken this text as license for first–trimester abortions since babies cannot be felt to kick in *utero* before the second trimester. Such Christians are living proof that the bare text of Scripture, apart from the interpretive Tradition of Christendom, says nothing clear and definite about abortion or human development anywhere. Instead, it gives *only* signs, clues, and hints, which individual Christians, forsaking that Tradition, can and do interpret in ways that directly contradict one another.

"Okay," the Evangelical says. "Maybe John the Baptist isn't a biblical pro-life proof, but what about our Lord Himself? Surely, the Personhood of the Second Person of the Trinity at His conception lends His dignity to all human beings from conception onward so that 'as you did it to one of the least of my brethren' (Mt 25:40) applies supremely here."

Though most Christians might agree with this argument, there are other well-meaning, Bible-believing Christians (most of them strongly pro-life) who don't. They see no such extension of Christ's dignity to us by the mere fact that Christ was born a human being. They note that Christ is speaking of the "least of *my* brethren" and argue that we become His brothers and God's children, not by being born but by being born *again*. They fear that to protect the unborn child on this basis is ultimately to mislead people into thinking we are holy when we are merely human.

Of course, there are counterarguments to all this, to which, of course, there are further counter-counterarguments till between the combatants you can't count the counters. But this is hardly evidence of the undeniable clarity of Scripture alone on this crucial point of Christian ethics.

Someone then might propose that the reason Scripture said so little was because abortion was unheard of at the time. After all, you don't pass laws against speeding if no one has yet invented the automobile. The difficulty with this theory is that it simply isn't true. Abortion predates Christianity by centuries, and it flourished in pagan culture then as it flourishes in our quasi-pagan culture now. That is why the *Didache*, a manual of Christian instruction composed around AD 80, during the lifetime of the Gospel writers, commands, "do not commit an abortion, nor kill anything that has been born,"[23] Nor was the *Didache* alone in this. The subsequent writings of the post-apostolic period are simply unanimous when it comes to the Christian teaching on this subject. *The Epistle of Barnabas*, the *Letter to Diognetus*, the writings of Athenagoras, Tertullian, Hippolytus, Origen, Epiphanius, Jerome, and a vast army of the Fathers — indeed every last Christian theologian who address-

---

23 Kenneth J. Howell, *Clement of Rome and the Didache* (Zanesville: CHResources, 2012), pp. 139–140.

es this question until late in this century says exactly the same thing: Abortion is a grave evil and the taking of human life.

Yet the odd thing is this: These ancient writers, the Fathers of the Church closest in time to the Apostles, speak of their doctrine both in this area and in many others as definitely decided by the mind of the Church and the Tradition of the Apostles. For them, abortion is contrary, not so much to the Bible, as to the Holy Faith they received from their predecessors. Thus Basil the Great (c. 374) writes: "A woman who has deliberately destroyed a fetus must pay the penalty for murder," and "Those also who give drugs causing abortions are murderers themselves, as well as those who receive the poison which kills the fetus."[24] Yet, for Basil, as for the rest of the Fathers, this teaching, like many others, has been preserved, not only in Scripture, but "in the Church." As he himself says:

> Of the dogmas and kerygmas preserved in the Church, some we possess from written teaching and others we receive from the tradition of the Apostles, handed on to us in mystery. In respect to piety both are of the same force. No one will contradict any of these, no one, at any rate, who is even moderately versed in matters ecclesiastical. Indeed, were we to try to reject unwritten customs as having no great authority, we would unwittingly injure the Gospel in its vitals.[25]

In short, the Faith of which the Fathers speak (including its pro-life ethic) is revealed, not merely by Scripture alone, but by *Scripture rightly understood (and only rightly understood) in the context of a larger Tradition that is just as much from God as the Scripture it interprets.*

---

24 St. Basil the Great, *Letter 188: To Amphilochius* 2, 8.

25 St. Basil the Great, *The Holy Spirit*, 27.66.

And no one, least of all Bible-alone Christians, questioned this pro-life teaching until this century. Indeed, the overwhelming number of Christians quite faithfully followed this teaching of Tradition without it even occurring to them to question it. Why was this, if they were truly deriving their beliefs from the clear and unambiguous teaching of the Bible alone, speaking forth only what Scripture spoke, keeping silent where Scripture was silent, and not binding the conscience of the believer on those questions in which Scripture permits different interpretations?

The obvious answer seems to be that this was a facet of extra-biblical Tradition which is so profoundly part of their bones that Christians never thought to distinguish it from (much less oppose it to) the Scriptures themselves. Indeed, *the total pro-life tradition is built upon Scripture and Tradition together*; distinct, yet an organic unity like the head and the heart, the right hand and the left. Scripture gives light, but a very scattered light on this most crucial of issues; *Tradition* acts like a lens bringing that dancing light into focus. Tradition without Scripture is a darkened lens without a light; but likewise, Scripture without Tradition is, on this vital issue, a blurry, unfocused light without a lens.

In a very real sense, Bible-alone Christians are no different from Catholic Christians on this score. Neither treat this teaching from Tradition— the Tradition of Pro-life Interpretation, one could call it — as a fallible human reading of Scripture; rather, both treat it as absolutely authoritative and therefore as *revealed*.

THE TRINITY

What could be more central to Evangelical Bible-only belief than the deity of Christ? This is the great thundering truth proclaimed by every good preacher of the gospel. If that is not essential Christianity, then there is no such thing as Christianity. Yet as one reads Scripture and examines Church history, it becomes clear that there are ways of denying the deity of Christ which can easily slip in under the Evangelical radar screen — ways which reverence Him and call loudly for trust in Scripture as the one and only source of revelation, yet which firmly consign Christ to the status of mere creature just as surely as does the most ardent skeptic. Most famous among these ways is a fourth–century movement known as Arianism.

Arians were principally concerned to preserve the oneness of God from pagan polytheism. They argued cogently from Scripture. They were well-trained theologians who could read Scripture in the original tongues. The only problem was that they had the idea that Jesus was not truly God but only a sort of godlet or superior created being.

In defense of this idea, the Arians rejected Tradition and pointed to texts like "the Father is greater than I" (Jn 14:28) and "Why do you call me good? No one is good but God alone" (Mk 10:18). They could come up with plausible explanations for terms and expressions which Evangelical Christians think could only point to Christ's divinity. For example, Arians said the statement, "I and the Father are one" (Jn 10:30) refers to oneness of *purpose*, not oneness of being. They pointed out that Scripture refers to supernatural created beings as "sons of God" (Job 38:7) without intending that they are one in being with the Father. They observed that even mere humans were called "gods" (Ps 82:6; Jn 10:34–36), without the implication that they are God. Therefore, they inferred that the Son, supernatural though He may be (as angels, principalities, and powers are supernatural), is neither co-eternal with the Father nor one in being with Him.

How can Christians argue against Arianism using Scripture alone? We might say that John speaks of the "only begotten" and says of Him that He "*was God*" and was "in the beginning *with God*" (Jn 1:18; 3:16; 1:1–2; emphasis added). We might also reply that, although the word Trinity is not in Scripture, nonetheless the *concept* of Trinity is there.

But a good Arian would be quick to point out that God plainly says, "You are my Son, today I have begotten you" (Heb 1:5), which implies that there was a time *before* the Son was begotten. In other words, the Arian can argue that there was a time when the Son was not. But there was never a time when the Father was not. He is without beginning. Therefore, according to the Arian, the Son does not share God's eternal, beginningless essence. This amounts to a denial of the deity of Christ. Great and supernatural as He may be compared to the rest of creation (and Paul implies He is a creature when he calls Him the firstborn of all *creation* [Col 1:15], doesn't he?), nonetheless He is *only* a creature, says the Arian.

How then can Bible-alone Christians even be sure of this foundation stone of the Faith if the ambiguity of Scripture makes it, too, a "matter of liberty," according to their own criteria?

The answer was given on one of those radio call-in shows where theologians tackle various questions about the Bible. The host of this show was a solid Evangelical who was always careful to speak of Scripture alone as the bottom line of revelation. Yet the odd thing was, when a particularly articulate exponent of anti-trinitarianism called and pointed out the typical Arian readings of various Scriptures, the host had one final bottom line *below* the bottom line. After citing various counter-Scriptures (and receiving more Arian readings by the caller until yet another stalemate seemed imminent), the host finally said, in essence, "Your interpretation is simply not what historic Christianity has ever understood its own Bible to mean." He then asked the Arian caller if he was really prepared to insist that twenty centuries of Christians (including people who had heard the Apostles with their own ears and who clearly regarded Jesus as God) had been utterly wrong about the central fact of their faith while he alone was right?

Is it plausible to wrench Scripture away from twenty centuries of ordinary Christian interpretation of so crucial a matter and declare the entire Church, from those who knew the Apostles down to the present, incapable of understanding what it meant in its own Scriptures concerning so fundamental an issue?

Is it even remotely likely that the entire early Church misunderstood the Apostles that badly? Is it not obvious that the churches preserved the plain apostolic meaning of the Scriptures by carrying in their bosom not only the text of Scripture, but the clear memory of the *way* the Apostles intended these texts to be understood? Was it not obvious that this living memory was, in fact, essential to correctly reading Scripture?

But in seeing this, isn't it also obvious that the Evangelical radio-show host (like most Christians) was saying that the Trinitarian interpretation living in the Church through Tradition was just as essential and revealed as the Scripture being interpreted? When Christians speak of the absolute union of the Father and the Son, they are in fact resting serenely, not on the Bible alone, but on the interpretative Tradition of the Church, just as Christianity rested serenely on Tradition regarding the sanctity of human life (and we could draw the same conclusions with regard to the teaching of Tradition on monogamy).

This means that regardless of what Bible-only Christians *say* about Tradition being "useful but not essential" to Christian revelation, they *behave* contrariwise with regard to the Trinity. In relying on a teaching founded in Tradition, united with and yet distinct from the Scripture it interprets, they behave exactly as though they believe that Tradition is the other leg upon which the revelation of Christ's deity stands.

It, therefore, is a plain mistake for Trinitarian pro-life Christians to think they speak forth only what Scripture speaks, keep silent where Scripture is silent, and never bind the conscience of the believer on those questions in which Scripture permits different interpretations. On the contrary, they live (and have to live) by Tradition almost as deeply as Catholics. For all faithful Christians, Tradition is the lens that focuses the light of Scripture. For all, that Tradition is not a pair of "useful but not necessary" disposable glasses; rather, it is the lens of our living eye and the heart of vision. It is so much a part of us that we are oblivious to it. Unfortunately, too many Christians have been so focused on the light of Scripture that they have forgotten the lens through which they look.

MARK P. SHEA *is a popular Catholic writer and speaker. Among other books, he has written* Making Senses Out of Scripture: Reading the Bible as the First Christians Did; By What Authority?: An Evangelical Discovers Catholic Tradition; *and* This is My Body: An Evangelical Discovers the Real Presence. *An award-winning columnist, he contributes numerous articles to many magazines. Mark also appears frequently on radio and TV. His website is mark-shea.com.*

9

DID THE CHURCH FATHERS BELIEVE IN *SOLA SCRIPTURA*?[26]

JOSEPH GALLEGOS

If the doctrine of sola Scriptura *is historically valid, then we should find evidence of it in the earliest Christian writings, those written concurrent with the documents that became what we call the New Testament, as well as those in the years following the close of the apostolic age. What did the disciples of the Apostles believe about the authority of Scripture alone apart from the authority of Tradition or the bishops of the Church?*

The Protestant Reformers themselves recognized the importance of this evidence for they often used quotes from antiquity to defend their views. As a result, many Protestants today presume that whatever our Lord taught His Apostles was totally contained within the writings of the New Testament, and the consequent faith of the earliest Christians was built upon the Bible alone; that the early Church Fathers affirmed both the material and formal sufficiency of Scripture; and that over time this was lost due to the corruption of the Catholic Church, until it was rediscovered in the sixteenth century by the Protestant Reformers.

For example, in an essay entitled "*sola Scriptura* and the Early Church," Protestant apologist William Webster argues

26 This is a revised version of an article by Joseph Gallegos that was previously published in the Coming Home Network International's *Sola Scriptura* journal. Reprinted with permission.

that the early Church Fathers were strong proponents of *sola Scriptura*. Mr. Webster writes:

> The Reformation was responsible for restoring to the Church the principle of *sola Scriptura*, a principle which had been operative within the Church from the very beginning of the post apostolic age. Initially the apostles taught orally but with the close of the apostolic age all special revelation that God wanted preserved for man was codified in the written Scriptures. *Sola Scriptura* is the teaching and belief that there is only one special revelation from God that man possesses today, the written Scriptures or the Bible, and that consequently the Scriptures are materially sufficient and are by their very nature as being inspired by God the ultimate authority for the Church.[27]

The mention of material and formal sufficiency calls for an explanation. *Sola Scriptura*, according to the Protestant Reformers' doctrine, consists of both a material and a formal element. First, *sola Scriptura* affirms that all doctrines of the Christian Faith are contained within the corpus of the Old and New Testaments. Hence, Scripture is materially sufficient. Second, *sola Scriptura* holds that Scripture requires no other co-ordinate authority, such as a teaching Church or Tradition, in order to determine its meaning, hence, the formal sufficiency of Scripture.

In the quote above, the Protestant apologist Mr. Webster equates *sola Scriptura* with the material sufficiency of Scripture. The Catholic Church has always affirmed Scripture's material sufficiency, but not its formal sufficiency. Webster, how-

---

27 This article is available online at http://christiananswers.net/q-eden/sola-scriptura-earlychurch.html.

ever, proceeds to claim that the Reformers were responsible for restoring this narrow understanding of *sola Scriptura*.

The question arises, therefore, did the early Church Fathers affirm both the material and formal sufficiency of Scripture? What I wish to demonstrate in this chapter is that, while the Fathers affirmed the material sufficiency, they did not accept the formal sufficiency; in fact they strongly confirmed the formal *insufficiency* of Scripture.

A thorough examination of this topic would require a much longer chapter, if not a book. However, to at least scratch the surface, let's begin with two of the earliest Christian Fathers who addressed this issue: St. Irenaeus and Tertullian. Some Protestant commentators have argued that these two early writers equated Tradition with Scripture, speaking of them interchangeably. For example, Webster states: "And there is no appeal in the writing of these fathers to a Tradition that is oral in nature for a defense of what they call Apostolic Tradition. The Apostolic Tradition for Irenaeus and Tertullian is simply Scripture."[28]

Both St. Irenaeus and Tertullian, however, understood Tradition as a substantive and coordinate authority alongside Scripture. These same Fathers believed that the doctrines of the Catholic Church are found in Tradition as well as in Scripture. They do not make the conclusion, though, that, since Tradition includes the same doctrines as Scripture, Tradition therefore is equated to Scripture.

The primary difference between Scripture and Tradition is that they convey the same teaching but through different mediums. One transmits the doctrines via the written Scriptures while Tradition transmits these same doctrines through the life, faith, and practice of the Church. If Scripture is equated with Tradition, then the writings of St. Irenaeus and Tertullian are reduced to nonsense.

28 Ibid.

St. Irenaeus writes as if he was anticipating proto-Protestants:

> When, however, they are confuted from the Scriptures, they turn round and accuse these same Scriptures, as if they were not correct, nor of authority, and [assert] that they are ambiguous, and that the truth cannot be extracted from them by those who are ignorant of tradition ... It comes to this, therefore, that these men do now consent neither to Scripture nor tradition.[29]

> Suppose there arise a dispute relative to some important question among us, should we not have recourse to the most ancient Churches with which the apostles held constant intercourse, and learn from them what is certain and clear in regard to the present question? For how should it be if the apostles themselves had not left us writings? Would it not be necessary, [in that case,] to follow the course of the tradition which they handed down to those to whom they did commit the Churches?[30]

According to Irenaeus, Tradition is substantive in content, normative in authority, and continues to live in the apostolic churches. Likewise Tertullian writes:

> Error of doctrine in the churches must necessarily have produced various issues. When, however, that which is deposited among many is found to be one and the same, it is not the result of error, but of tradition. Can any one, then, be reckless

---

29 St. Irenaeus, *Against Heresies*, 3,2:1.
30 Ibid., 3,4:1.

enough to say that they were in error who handed
on the tradition?[31]

First, St. Irenaeus and Tertullian had no issue with the concept of an authoritative Tradition alongside Scripture. What
they criticized was that the Gnostics' tradition was private
and available only to the Gnostic elect in contrast to a Tradition that was public, aboveboard, taught, and preserved by the
Catholic Church. This was the point that was foisted in the
face of the Gnostics by St. Irenaeus and Tertullian:

> But, again, when we refer them to that tradition
> which originates from the apostles, [and] which is
> preserved by means of the successions of presby-
> ters in the Churches, they object to tradition, say-
> ing they themselves are wiser.[32]

> His testimony, therefore, is true, and the doc-
> trine of the apostles is open and steadfast, holding
> nothing in reserve; nor did they teach one set of
> doctrines in private, and another in public.[33]

> [The Apostles] next went forth into the world and
> preached the same doctrine of the same faith to the
> nations. They then in like manner rounded church-
> es in every city, from which all the other churches,
> one after another, derived the tradition of the faith,
> and the seeds of doctrine, and are every day deriv-
> ing them, that they may become churches. Indeed,
> it is on this account only that they will be able to
> deem themselves apostolic, as being the offspring
> of apostolic churches. Every sort of thing must
> necessarily revert to its original for its classifica-

---

31 Tertullian, *The Prescription against Heretics*, 28.

32 St. Irenaeus, *Against Heresies*, 3,2:2.

33 Ibid., 3,15:1.

tion. Therefore the churches, although they are so many and so great, comprise but the one primitive church, (founded) by the apostles, from which they all (spring). In this way all are primitive, and all are apostolic, whilst they are all proved to be one, in (unbroken) unity, by their peaceful communion and title of brotherhood, and bond of hospitality, — privileges which no other rule directs than the one tradition of the selfsame mystery.[34]

Ellen Flessman-Van Leer, a non-Catholic scholar, has written in depth and without equivocation on St. Irenaeus' and Tertullian's understanding of Apostolic Tradition: "For Irenaeus, on the other hand, tradition and scripture are both quite unproblematic. They stand independently side by side, both absolutely authoritative, both unconditionally true, trustworthy, and convincing."[35]

Elsewhere Van Leer comments on Tertullian:

Tertullian says explicitly that the apostles delivered their teaching both orally and later on through epistles, and the whole body of this teaching he designates with the word traditio ...This is tradition in the real sense of the word. It is used for the original message of the apostles, going back to revelation, and for the message proclaimed by the church, which has been received through the apostles.[36]

Van Leer concludes:

---

34 Tertullian, *The Prescription against Heretics,* 20.
35 Ellen Flessman-Van Leer, *Tradition and Scripture in the Early Church* (Assen: Van Gorcum, 1953), p. 139.
36 Ibid., pp. 146, 147, 168.

Irenaeus and Tertullian point to the church tradition as the authoritative locus of the unadulterated
teaching of the apostles, they can no longer appeal
to the immediate memory, as could the earliest
writers. Instead they lay stress on the affirmation
that this teaching has been transmitted faithfully
from generation to generation. One could say that
in their thinking, apostolic succession occupies
the same place that is held by the living memory
in the Apostolic Fathers.[37]

J.N.D. Kelly, an Anglican patristic scholar, confirms this
view:

It should be unnecessary to accumulate further
evidence. Throughout the whole period Scripture
and tradition ranked as complementary authori-
ties, media different in form but coincident in
content. To inquire which counted as superior or
more ultimate is to pose the question in mislead-
ing terms. If Scripture was abundantly sufficient
in principle, tradition was recognized as the sur-
est clue to its interpretation, for in tradition the
Church retained, as a legacy from the apostles
which was embedded in all the organs of her insti-
tutional life, an unerring grasp of the real purport
and meaning of the revelation to which Scripture
and tradition alike bore witness.[38]

There are a couple of recurring themes throughout the
writings of the Church Fathers on the rule of faith.

First, the Fathers affirmed that the most perfect expression
of the apostolic faith is to be found in Sacred Scripture. The

---

37   Ibid., p. 188.

38   J.N.D. Kelly, *Early Christian Doctrines* (New York: HarperOne, 1978), pp. 47–48.

Fathers, therefore, affirmed the material sufficiency of Scripture. According to the Fathers, all doctrines of the Catholic Faith are to be found within its covers.

Secondly, the Fathers affirmed in the same breath and with equal conviction that the apostolic Faith has also been transmitted to the Church through Tradition. According to the Fathers, the Scriptures can be interpreted only within the Catholic Church in light of her Sacred Tradition. The Fathers, particularly those who combated heresies, affirmed that the fatal flaw of heretics was interpreting Scripture according to their private understanding apart from Mother Church and her Tradition. The Fathers, therefore, argued against any formal sufficiency of Scripture.

In sum, when the Fathers affirmed the sufficiency and authority of Scripture, they did so not in a vacuum, but within the framework of an authoritative Church and Tradition. Let me cite passages:

St. Cyril of Jerusalem (c. AD 315–386), Doctor of the Catholic Church and bishop, writes: "But in learning the Faith and in professing it, acquire and keep that only, which is now delivered to thee by the Church, and which has been built up strongly out of all the Scripture."[39] Here we see St. Cyril's clear Catholic understanding of the rule of faith. Elsewhere, St. Cyril points to the Church, not to Scripture, for the definition of the canon: "Learn also diligently, and from the Church, what are the books of the Old Testament, and what those of the New."[40]

St. Gregory of Nyssa (c. AD 335–394), brother of St. Basil the Great, Doctor of the Catholic Church, and bishop of Nyssa, writes:

> [F]or it is enough for proof of our statement, that the tradition has come down to us from our fa-

---

39 St. Cyril of Jerusalem, *Catechetical Lectures*, 5:12.
40 Ibid., 4:33.

thers, handed on, like some inheritance, by succession from the apostles and the saints who came after them. They, on the other hand, who change their doctrines to this novelty, would need the support of arguments in abundance, if they were about to bring over to their views, not men light as dust, and unstable, but men of weight and steadiness: but so long as their statement is advanced without being established, and without being proved, who is so foolish and so brutish as to account the teaching of the evangelists and apostles, and of those who have successively shone like lights in the churches, of less force than this undemonstrated nonsense?[41]

St. Basil the Great (AD 329–379), Doctor of the Catholic Church, bishop of Caesarea, and brother of St. Gregory of Nyssa, writes:

Of the dogmas and kergymas preserved in the Church, some we possess from written teaching and others we receive from the tradition of the Apostles, handed on to us in mystery. In respect to piety both are of the same force. No one will contradict any of these, no one, at any rate, who is even moderately versed in manners ecclesiastical. Indeed, were we to try to reject the unwritten customs as having no great authority, we would unwittingly injure the Gospel in its vitals; or rather, we would reduce kergyma to a mere term.[42]

It would be easy for anyone to cut and paste the Fathers to their liking; however, to find the authentic faith of a Fa-

---

41 St. Gregory of Nyssa, *Against Eunomius*, 4:6 (emphasis added).
42 St. Basil the Great, *Of the Holy Spirit*, 27:66.

ther we must look at their entire writings. It is clear that the early Church Fathers appealed to Tradition alongside Scripture. This Tradition was normative, substantive, available to all, and preserved by the apostolic churches, particularly the See of Rome.

JOSEPH GALLEGOS *is the author of the chapter "What Did the Church Fathers Teach about Scripture, Tradition, and Church Authority" in the book* Not by Scripture Alone *(Queenship Publishing, 1997). His website www.cin.org/users/jgallegos/contents.htm is devoted to the teachings of the Church Fathers.*

10

ST. AUGUSTINE AND *SOLA SCRIPTURA*[43]

DR. KENNETH HOWELL

St. Augustine of Hippo (AD 354–430) ranks not only among the greatest Fathers and Doctors of the Church but also as the preeminent Father in the West: his influence on Western history has been unparalleled. At the time of the Protestant Reformation, all the major theologies in Christendom appealed to his authority: Catholics, Lutherans, and Reformed. John Calvin, for example, appealed to Augustine as a secondary support for his doctrines and interpretations of Scripture as did his greatest Catholic critic, Cardinal Robert Bellarmine.

It would not be an exaggeration to say that the theological issues of the Protestant Reformation were as much about the writings of St. Augustine as they were about the Bible. In light of his importance, it is worth asking what St. Augustine thought about the authority of Scripture.

Augustine's preeminence in the Western Church is only matched by his prolific output. While maintaining a busy life as bishop, preacher, reconciler, and disciple, he left us more than any other writer of antiquity: over five million words. Yet

---

43 This is a revised version of an article written by Dr. Kenneth Howell that was originally published in the Coming Home Network International's August 2014 newsletter. Reprinted with permission.

in all these words the issue of *sola Scriptura* never arose. As far as I am aware, Augustine never addressed the issue as it was formulated in the Protestant Reformation. He did, however, reflect on the authority of Scripture, especially the authority of various interpretations of Scripture, so that his reflections can be relevant to the issue of *sola Scriptura* in the modern world.

DID ST. AUGUSTINE BELIEVE IN *SOLA SCRIPTURA*?

Because Augustine held the Scriptures in high esteem and venerated them as an inerrant authority for the Church, many Protestant theologians and apologists have quoted him as a support for the notion of *sola Scriptura*. In his famous *Letter to Jerome* (ca. 405), Augustine says:

> I have learned to yield this respect and honor only to the canonical books of Scripture: of these alone do I most firmly believe that the authors were completely free from error. And if in these writings I am perplexed by anything which appears to me opposed to truth, I do not hesitate to suppose that either the manuscript is faulty, or the translator has not caught the meaning of what was said, or I myself have failed to understand it.[44]

Augustine goes on to contrast this infallible authority of the canonical Scriptures with other writings about the same subjects:

> As to all other writings, in reading them, however great the superiority of the authors to myself in sanctity and learning, I do not accept their teaching as true on the mere ground of the opinion being held by them; but only because they have succeeded in convincing my judgment of its truth

44 St. Augustine, *Letter to Jerome*, no. 82.

either by means of these canonical writings themselves, or by arguments addressed to my reason.

Advocates of *sola Scriptura* like to point out that Augustine
even uses the Protestant phrase in the first sentence (*solis eis
Scripturarum libris* "to the books of Scripture alone") which
supports their contention that the great bishop of Hippo em-
braced *sola Scriptura*.

This is a case where careful reading of documents is of par-
amount importance. The contexts of Augustine's comments
and those of Reformers in the sixteenth century are quite
different, not only in time, but in substance. Protestants con-
trasted the absolute authority of Scripture and what they considered the unjust authority of Tradition or the Magisterium
of the Church. For them, the Scriptures alone were the proper
source from which Christian doctrine and morals should be
extracted. To add the authority of the Church was to undermine God's authority by adding human authority to it. But
in Augustine's arguments with Jerome ten centuries earlier,
the issue was not about the authority of the canonical Scriptures taken as a whole — Jerome himself affirmed that — but
whether one should allow historical mistakes within Scripture.
When Paul writes of Peter in Galatians 2:14 that he did not act
in accord with "the truth of the gospel," Jerome had supposed
that Paul had made a mistake in his writing. Augustine, in the
quotations above, is affirming that the Scriptures are inerrant,
not that they are the sole authority. Other writings may err but
not the Scriptures.

Still, a Protestant may say that even this lesser affirmation
by Augustine means that he believed that Church Tradition,
writings of the Fathers, and Church councils could err while
the Scriptures alone could not. They therefore could be the
only source of absolute truth for the Church. So the Protestant
Reformers saw themselves as justified in appealing to Augus-

tine. And if one limits himself to a few select quotations from Augustine's writings, that may seem to be true, a fact which would explain how generations of Protestants could see themselves as faithful to the bishop of Hippo.

sola Scriptura as a Problem of Interpretation Many contemporary apologists, both Catholic and Protestant, have limited their debate about the sole authority of Scripture to affirmations or denials about the Scriptures taken as a whole, prior to any interpretation by an individual or the Church. In this framing of the question, Catholic apologists often cite Church Fathers who affirm the necessity of both Scripture and Tradition. And there is an abundance of such texts to be had. Augustine, however, did not face the problem in that form. Rather, his life and work had more to do with *how to interpret the Scriptures in the light of schisms and heresies all around him.* Three examples in his lifetime were Manicheanism, Donatism, and what may be called simplistic literalism.

In his disputes with Faustus the Manichean bishop, Augustine insisted on the absolute authority of the canonical Scriptures against Faustus' claim that there were later writings of equal authority.

> The excellence of the canonical authority of the Old and New Testaments is distinct from the books of later writers. This authority was confirmed in the times of the Apostles through the succession of bishops and the propagation of churches, as if it was settled in a heavenly manner in a kind of seat to which every believing and pious mind lives in obedience.[45]

Attending carefully to the wording of this statement reveals three important truths in Augustine's thinking.

45 St. Augustine, *Against Faustus*, 11:5.

1. Manichean writings ("books of later writers") cannot be held as of equal authority with the Bible because they lack the confirmation of the historic Church ("through the succession of bishops and the propagation of churches"). Here Augustine says that the Church is the protector of Scripture's integrity.

2. When he invokes the imagery of a seat, Augustine means the Church as an authority. It is to this seat that every believing Christian must live in obedience.

3. While the Scriptures rightly command the assent and obedience of every Christian, the same Scriptures can only be known by their derivation from and connection with the historic Church.

The Donatist controversy was very different. On the surface, the Donatist controversy does not seem to have anything to do with the authority of Scripture. Here the issue was schism from the Catholic Church. By the time Augustine arrived on the scene of history, the Donatist schism in North Africa was over a century old. What is striking is that most of what the Donatists taught was in accord with Catholic teaching; their great sin was separation or schism. Yet, on at least one crucial doctrinal point, they differed from the Catholics. They wanted to remain separated from the Church because they considered its sacraments invalid. Why invalid? The ministers of the Catholic Church were tainted with sin and apostasy. The Donatist insisted that a priest who conferred Baptism but was himself not a good man could not confer the forgiveness of sins. His immoral life invalidated his sacramental ministry. Augustine's answer was multifaceted, but on one point he was crystal clear. The Scriptures teach that Baptism confers forgiveness even if the man baptizing is himself an immoral man.

> But I think that we have sufficiently shown, both
> from the canon of Scripture, and from the letters
> of Cyprian himself, that bad men, while not con-
> verted to a better mind, were able to, and in fact
> do confer, and receive baptism, of these it is most
> clear that they do not belong to the holy Church of
> God, though they seem to be within it.[46]

This quotation is significant not only because of what it reveals about the meaning of Baptism but also about scriptural
authority. The objective validity of Baptism cannot be nulli-
fied by a sinful man. As Augustine says, this truth he demonstrated from the Scriptures. Further, while the Donatists were
appealing to the teaching of St. Cyprian, Augustine showed
that the earlier bishop's teaching was not really being upheld
by the schismatics. In other words, Augustine sought to read
the scriptural meaning of Baptism through the prism of the
Church prior to his time. Schism from the Church was associated with schism from the Church's understanding of Scripture.

The third problem St. Augustine faced was not really her-
esy or schism but the difficulties which "the little ones" had in
understanding the Scriptures. In *On Christian Doctrine*, Augustine's most theoretical discussion of interpretation, he sug-
gests that interpretation of scriptural passages should attempt
to discern the intention of the biblical author. This meant pay-
ing careful attention to the contexts of the text, both immediate and remote, comparing text with text, but it also meant
adhering to the rule of faith:

> Let the reader consult the rule of faith which he has
> gathered from the plainer passages of Scripture,
> and from the authority of the Church, and of which
> I treated at sufficient length when I was speaking in
> the first book about things. But if both readings,

46 St. Augustine, *On Baptism, Against the Donatists*, 6:3.

or all of them (if there are more than two), give a meaning in harmony with the faith, it remains to consult the context, both what goes before and what comes after, to see which interpretation, out of many that offer themselves, it pronounces for and permits to be dovetailed into itself.[47]

Here Augustine emphasizes that in cases of doubt about the meaning of a scriptural text, one should seek to discern "the rule of faith" from the Scriptures and from "the authority of the Church." The importance in adhering to the Faith handed down (Tradition) is emphasized by Augustine elsewhere. In *On Marriage and Concupiscence*, he discusses original sin and contrasts "the most ancient and firm rule of the catholic faith" with "those who assert new and perverse doctrines." His appeal is ultimately to the ancient faith transmitted through the Church, because it "suits all hearts in the catholic Church and appeals to the very faith which has been firmly established and transmitted from ancient times with unfaltering voice."

Augustine walked a fine line between too little and too much latitude. In his *Literal Commentary on Genesis*, he insisted that a Christian should allow differing interpretations when the text seemed obscure. To be too narrow was to sin against charity.[48] On the other hand, too much latitude in interpretation risked putting oneself outside the Faith. But how does one know what is too much or too little? Augustine's answer lies in the rule of faith and the authority of the Church, both of which meant a humble listening to the past wisdom of the Church.

When Luther, Calvin, and other Protestants began to emphasize *sola Scriptura*, they believed that the Catholic Church had not only gone astray in the behavior of its members —

---

47 St. Augustine, *On Christian Doctrine*, 3:2.

48 Cf. *Confessions*, bk. 12.

something true in every generation — but also in its doctrines. The source of those doctrinal errors, according to the Reformers, was placing Church Tradition above the authority of Scripture. This they held to be the root cause of the Catholic Church's departure from the Faith. Had the Protestant Reformers understood St. Augustine better, they would have had more charity toward the Church in their interpretations and more fidelity to the ancient Faith.

DR. KENNETH HOWELL *is a former Presbyterian pastor and professor of theology who was received into the Catholic Church in 1996. Dr. Howell has authored dozens of articles and seven books, including* Something Greater Is Here; Ignatius of Antioch and Polycarp of Smyrna: A New Translation and Theological Commentary; *and* Clement of Rome and the Didache: A New Translation and Theological Commentary.

11

AN AUTHORITY WE CAN TRUST[49]

REV. DWIGHT LONGENECKER

So far in this short book, we have tried to demonstrate that the Scriptures, though inspired, were never intended to be alone. A mere examination of history illustrates that sola Scriptura *could not have been God's plan for the spread of the Gospel, especially in the early centuries of the Church. The Scriptures themselves do not promote* sola Scriptura, *and the proliferation of denominations, divided primarily over the interpretation of Scripture, is a strong argument against the perspicuity of Scripture, as well as the accuracy of private interpretation. The Scriptures, along with the witness of the early Church Fathers, point to the importance of standing firm on the fullness of the Apostolic Tradition, as delivered by Christ to His Apostles and then passed on, primarily through oral teaching and preaching, but also in written form — the occasion of these written addendum to the Apostolic Tradition were generally because the author was prevented from getting to his intended audience to deliver his message orally in person.*

We also recognize, however, that there were many other books and challenging teachings arising during the time of the New Testament Scriptures and the early Church Fathers. Since

---

49 This is a revised version of an article written by Rev. Dwight Longenecker originally titled "What Is Truth? An Examination of *Sola Scriptura*" that was part of his apologetics series for London's Premier Radio. Reprinted with permission.

there was no infallible, inspired list or canon as to which of these many books were to be considered *Scripture*, the bishops of the Church were guided by the Holy Spirit in Council to make this decision. And as competing ideas arose challenging orthodox theology, the leaders of the Church looked to Scripture as interpreted by the traditions passed down in the churches of the Apostles to determine which were true.

But throughout all the centuries of Christianity, how was the average Christian to know what was true? How was the average layman, who through most of history could not read, or the local priest, who was ordained to lead him, to determine what was necessary to believe and do, or not do, to be saved? As mentioned in Chapter 3 above, as pondered by that minister named Stephen, the answer is in that thought: *The Church ... the pillar ... the bulwark ... the truth.*

As the Apostle Paul instructed his apprentice bishop, Timothy: "I hope to come to you soon, but I am writing these instructions to you so that, if I am delayed, you may know how one ought to behave in the household of God, which is the Church of the living God, the pillar and bulwark of the truth" (1 Tim 3:14–15).

In Ephesians 3:10, Paul likewise taught that it was God's intent "that through the Church the manifold wisdom of God might now be made known."

In other words, it is through the Church that we learn the truth about Jesus — not just through the Bible. It is by belonging to the living body of Christ — the Church — that we come to understand and know the mystery of Jesus Christ Himself.

Paul says that the Church is the *pillar and foundation of truth*. So the Church is the basis and the support for the truth. It is on the Church that the whole edifice rests and is supported. It's no exaggeration to say then that not only did the Church establish and validate the inspiration of the Bible, and determine which specific books were to be considered inspired Scripture, but that without the Church we wouldn't have a Bible at all.

THE GUIDANCE OF THE HOLY SPIRIT

These convictions are based on the belief that Jesus always keeps His promises. He promised that He would send the Holy Spirit upon His Apostles to guide them into all truth (Jn 16:13). He also promised that He would be with His followers forever (Mt 28:20; cf. Jn 14:16). As a result, the Church has always believed that she carries the responsibility of preserving and protecting the truth as handed down from Jesus through His Apostles, in both written and oral form. And this Spirit of Pentecost is still poured out on the Church — guiding and protecting and teaching.

Some, however, may point with confidence to the First Letter of John when the Apostle assured his disciples: "You have been anointed by the Holy One, and you all know. I write to you, not because you do not know the truth, but because you know it, and know that no lie is of the truth.... The anointing which you received from him abides in you, and you have no need that any one should teach you" (1 Jn 2:20–21, 27).

Therefore, they claim that have no need of a Church to teach them; they have the Holy Spirit within them. They claim that they are not making *any private interpretation of Scripture*, as Peter warned in his Second Letter, but are interpreting it through the Holy Spirit. But this is not what either of the Apostles meant: the Apostles were using their apostolic authority to correct their Spirit-filled hearers' sometimes erroneous interpretations.

In 2 Peter 1:16–18, Peter claimed teaching authority because he was an eyewitness of Jesus' life and glory, and received the truth directly from Jesus. He then indicates in 3:2 that the truth of God which was once delivered by the holy prophets was now given through the Apostles.

What is important to see here is that Peter compares the role of the New Testament Apostles to the Old Testament prophets. God directly inspired the prophets. Their preaching was considered to be a direct word from God to the people of God. The Apostles, chosen and empowered by Christ, are the God-inspired teachers of the New Testament people of God. When Peter says, "No prophecy of Scripture is a matter of one's own interpretation" (2 Pet 1:20), he means that only the prophet of God — that is, the Apostle — is entitled and empowered by the Holy Spirit to give the right interpretation.

Paul agrees with him. In Ephesians 3:5, he says that "the mystery of Christ ... has now been revealed to his holy apostles and prophets by the Spirit." And it is this same Spirit-led group of men who are the foundation of the Church. So Paul says in 2:20 that the Ephesians are members of the Church, "the household of God, built upon the foundation of the apostles and prophets, Christ Jesus himself being the cornerstone." Jesus is the cornerstone of this Church, but it is the Apostles and the prophets — inspired by God's Holy Spirit — who provide the foundation for the Church (cf. Rev 21:14).

This verse fits together with Paul's other teaching that the Church is the "pillar and foundation of truth" (1 Tim 3:15, NAB). So the Church — based on the teaching of the Apostles, inspired to write the Scriptures, and inspired to choose which books were to be included in the Bible, is also its chosen, Spirit-filled interpreter of Scripture.

WHERE DOES ONE FIND
THIS APOSTOLIC CHURCH TODAY?

If it's true that the Apostles were the ones to interpret Scripture, and the apostolic Church was therefore the one to interpret Scripture, does that same apostolic authority exist today? If so, where can we find it?

We have seen that Paul explicitly handed on his teaching authority to Timothy and commanded him to hand that authority on to others, who would in turn hand it on to their successors (2 Tim 2:2). But Timothy wasn't the only one. Paul also sent Titus to Crete to establish the Church there. Calling Titus his son in the faith, he said, "This is why I left you in Crete, that you might amend what was defective, and appoint elders in every town as I directed you" (Titus 1:5). And what kind of a man must this presbyter be? "He must hold firm to the sure word as taught, so that he may be able to give instruction in sound doctrine and also to confute those who contradict it" (1:9). So in the New Testament, we see Paul clearly setting up the Church with his sons in the faith as his successors in the various locations.

The writings of the early Church testify that the first generation of Christians after the Apostles believed their Church leaders had somehow inherited the same teaching authority that the Apostles had.

So Clement, the bishop of Rome, around AD 95 writes:

> The apostles received the gospel for us from our Lord Jesus Christ, and Jesus Christ was sent from God … Once they received commands, once they were made confident through the resurrection of our Lord Jesus Christ, and once they were entrusted with God's word, they went out proclaiming with the confidence of the Holy Spirit that the kingdom of God would come. Preaching in lands and cities, by spiritual discernment, they began establishing their first fruits, who were bishops and deacons for future believers.… Our apostles knew from our Lord Jesus Christ that there would be

contention over the title of the bishop's office. For this reason, having received perfect foreknowledge, they appointed those mentioned before and afterwards gave the provision that, if they should fall asleep, other approved men would succeed their ministry.[50]

So Clement of Rome believed that the Apostles — one of whom, John, may still have been alive — had wished for their teaching office to be continued in the Church.

Ignatius of Antioch was martyred about the year AD 107. In writing to the Trallian Church, he equates the Church presbyters with Apostles: "As is already your practice, it is necessary to do nothing without [the approval] of the bishop, but to be submissive to the presbytery as to the apostles of Jesus Christ, our hope. We will be found in him if we spend our lives for him."[51]

And Irenaeus, who wrote around AD 180, also believed firmly that the Church had inherited the authority of the Apostles to teach the truth faithfully. According to him, it is because the Church leaders have inherited the apostolic authority that they can interpret Scripture properly. So he writes,

> By knowledge of the truth we mean: the teaching of the Apostles; the order of the Church as established from earliest times throughout the world ... preserved through the episcopal succession: for to the bishops the Apostles committed the care of the Church in each place which has come down to our own time safeguarded by ... the most complete exposition ... the reading of the Scriptures without falsification and careful and consistent

50 Kenneth Howell, *Clement of Rome and the Didache* (Zanesville: CHResources, 2012), pp. 115, 117.

51 Kenneth Howell, *Ignatius of Antioch and Polycarp of Smyrna* (Zanesville: CHResources, 2009), pp. 103–104.

exposition of them — avoiding both rashness and blasphemy.[52]

Remembering that Paul handed on his teaching authority to Timothy and Titus, and seeing how through history that authority has been handed down from generation to generation, Catholics believe that the dynamic and living teaching authority continues to live within the Catholic bishops who have received their ministry in direct line from the Apostles, passed down over the last two thousand years. As Pope St. John Paul II wrote in his opening line of the *Catechism of the Catholic Church*, "Guarding the deposit of faith is the mission which the Lord entrusted to His Church."[53]

Because of this direct link, Catholics believe the Church has a living connection with the apostolic authority, and that within the living Apostolic Tradition of the Catholic Church we can find a rock-solid, sure, historic, and unified body of teaching which illuminates and interprets the Bible without fail.

---

52 Henry Bettenson, *The Early Christian Fathers*, (Oxford: Oxford University Press, 1969), p. 89.

53 *Catechism of the Catholic Church*, 2nd. ed. (Washington, DC: United States Catholic Conference, 2000), p. 1.

12

WHAT *DOES* THE CATHOLIC CHURCH TEACH ABOUT SCRIPTURE?

If one is to at least consider the possibility that "the church of the living God" — which Paul said is "the pillar and bulwark of the truth" — subsists[54] or continues in the Catholic Church, then what does the Catholic Church teach about Scripture and how to correctly interpret it?

As with other doctrines, non-Catholics rarely take the time to read what the Catholic Church truly teaches about the inerrancy and authority of Scripture. Far too often, non-Catholics accept uncritically what anti-Catholics claim that Catholics believe. Let's say that you are a Baptist. You hear that the local Catholic church is giving a class on what Baptists believe. Would you be pleased if you also heard that the instructor was an ex-Baptist who now hates the Baptist church and is using as a textbook the book he wrote against the Baptist church? Likewise, isn't it only fair and sensible that we examine, from documents written or endorsed by the Church, what the Catholic Church herself teaches about Scripture, Tradition, and its teaching authority?

But where does one go for this? There are no churches in the world that have more official historical documents than the Catholic Church, so at first the goal may seem daunting. True, with modern technology, it has never been easier for

54 *Lumen Gentium*, no. 8.

anyone in the world to access and read these — and *for free!* Many sites online give direct access to all the encyclicals of the popes and all the documents from all the official Church councils. But the question remains, where does one go, because sometimes a wealth of information can be paralyzing?

The one best and most up-to-date, reliable source for hearing what the Catholic Church truly believes and teaches is the *Catechism of the Catholic Church* (*CCC*). This is precisely what Pope St. John Paul II proclaimed in his Apostolic Constitution *Fidei Depositum* (On the Publication of the Catechism of the Catholic Church):

> *The Catechism of the Catholic Church*, which I approved 25 June last and the publication of which I today order by virtue of my Apostolic Authority, is a statement of the Church's faith and of catholic doctrine, attested to or illumined by Sacred Scripture, the Apostolic Tradition and the Church's Magisterium. I declare it to be a sure norm for teaching the faith and thus a valid and legitimate instrument for ecclesial communion. May it serve the renewal to which the Holy Spirit ceaselessly calls the Church of God, the Body of Christ, on her pilgrimage to the undiminished light of the Kingdom![55]

I strongly encourage every Christian — every person — to take the time (at least once in a lifetime!) to read through the *Catechism* from start to finish. This will give you a sense of the unity and flow of the Church's teaching on these and other matters. Specifically, paragraphs 74 through 141 cover what the Catholic Church teaches on Scripture, the Apostolic Tradition, the Deposit of Faith, and the authority behind how Scripture is to be interpreted. (It is significant to note that these

---

55 *CCC*, no. 3.

paragraphs appear in the beginning of the *Catechism* — which consists of 2,865 paragraphs — indicating the prime importance of these matters in the outline of the Catholic Faith.) For your convenience and trustworthy reflection, we are presenting these paragraphs below:

PART ONE: THE PROFESSION OF FAITH
SECTION ONE: "I BELIEVE" — "WE BELIEVE"
CHAPTER TWO: GOD COMES TO MEET MAN

ARTICLE 2: THE TRANSMISSION OF DIVINE REVELATION

74 God "desires all men to be saved and to come to the knowledge of the truth":[56] that is, of Christ Jesus.[57] Christ must be proclaimed to all nations and individuals, so that this revelation may reach to the ends of the earth:

> God graciously arranged that the things he had once revealed for the salvation of all peoples should remain in their entirety, throughout the ages, and be transmitted to all generations.[58]

I. THE APOSTOLIC TRADITION

75 "Christ the Lord, in whom the entire Revelation of the most high God is summed up, commanded the apostles to preach the Gospel, which had been promised beforehand by the prophets, and which he fulfilled in his own person and promulgated with his own lips. In preaching the Gospel, they were to communicate the gifts of God to all men. This Gospel was to be the source of all saving truth and moral discipline.[59]

---

56 1 *Tim* 2:4.

57 Cf. *Jn* 14:6.

58 *DV* 7; cf. *2 Cor* 1:20; 3:16–4:6.

59 *DV* 7; cf. *Mt* 28:19–20; *Mk* 16:15.

In the apostolic preaching…

76 In keeping with the Lord's command, the Gospel was handed on in two ways:

— *orally* "by the apostles who handed on, by the spoken word of their preaching, by the example they gave, by the institutions they established, what they themselves had received — whether from the lips of Christ, from his way of life and his works, or whether they had learned it at the prompting of the Holy Spirit";[60]

— *in writing* "by those apostles and other men associated with the apostles who, under the inspiration of the same Holy Spirit, committed the message of salvation to writing".[61]

…continued in apostolic succession

77 "In order that the full and living Gospel might always be preserved in the Church the apostles left bishops as their successors. They gave them 'their own position of teaching authority.'"[62] Indeed, "the apostolic preaching, which is expressed in a special way in the inspired books, was to be preserved in a continuous line of succession until the end of time."[63]

78 This living transmission, accomplished in the Holy Spirit, is called Tradition, since it is distinct from Sacred Scripture, though closely connected to it. Through Tradition, "the Church, in her doctrine, life and worship perpetuates and transmits to every generation all that she herself is, all that she believes."[64] "The sayings of the holy Fathers are a witness to the life-giving presence of this Tradition, show-

---

60 *DV* 7.
61 *DV* 7.
62 *DV* 7 § 2; St. Irenaeus, *Adv. haeres.* 3, 3, 1:PG 7, 848; Harvey, 2, 9.
63 *DV* 8 § 1.
64 *DV* 8 § 1.

ing how its riches are poured out in the practice and life of the Church, in her belief and her prayer."[65]

79 The Father's self-communication made through his Word in the Holy Spirit, remains present and active in the Church: "God, who spoke in the past, continues to converse with the Spouse of his beloved Son. And the Holy Spirit, through whom the living voice of the Gospel rings out in the Church — and through her in the world — leads believers to the full truth, and makes the Word of Christ dwell in them in all its richness."[66]

II. THE RELATIONSHIP BETWEEN TRADITION AND SACRED SCRIPTURE

One common source...

80 "Sacred Tradition and Sacred Scripture, then, are bound closely together and communicate one with the other. For both of them, flowing out from the same divine wellspring, come together in some fashion to form one thing and move towards the same goal."[67] Each of them makes present and fruitful in the Church the mystery of Christ, who promised to remain with his own "always, to the close of the age".[68]

...two distinct modes of transmission

81 "*Sacred Scripture* is the speech of God as it is put down in writing under the breath of the Holy Spirit."[69]

"And [Holy] *Tradition* transmits in its entirety the Word of God which has been entrusted to the apostles by Christ the Lord and the Holy Spirit. It transmits it to the successors of the apostles so that, enlightened by the Spirit of truth, they

---

65 *DV* 8 § 3.

66 *DV* 8 § 3; cf. *Col* 3:16.

67 *DV* 9.

68 *Mt* 28:20.

69 *DV* 9.

may faithfully preserve, expound and spread it abroad by their preaching."[70]

82 As a result the Church, to whom the transmission and interpretation of Revelation is entrusted, "does not derive her certainty about all revealed truths from the holy Scriptures alone. Both Scripture and Tradition must be accepted and honored with equal sentiments of devotion and reverence."[71]

Apostolic Tradition and ecclesial traditions

83 The Tradition here in question comes from the apostles and hands on what they received from Jesus' teaching and example and what they learned from the Holy Spirit. The first generation of Christians did not yet have a written New Testament, and the New Testament itself demonstrates the process of living Tradition.

Tradition is to be distinguished from the various theological, disciplinary, liturgical or devotional traditions, born in the local churches over time. These are the particular forms, adapted to different places and times, in which the great Tradition is expressed. In the light of Tradition, these traditions can be retained, modified or even abandoned under the guidance of the Church's Magisterium.

III. THE INTERPRETATION OF THE HERITAGE OF FAITH

The heritage of faith entrusted to the whole of the Church

84 The apostles entrusted the "Sacred deposit" of the faith (the *depositum fidei*),[72] contained in Sacred Scripture and Tradition, to the whole of the Church. "By adhering to [this heritage] the entire holy people, united to its pastors, remains always faithful to the teaching of the apostles, to the

---

70 *DV* 9.

71 *DV* 9.

72 *DV* 10 § 1; cf. 1 *Tim* 6:20; 2 *Tim* 1:12–14 (Vulg.).

brotherhood, to the breaking of bread and the prayers. So, in maintaining, practicing, and professing the faith that has been handed on, there should be a remarkable harmony between the bishops and the faithful."[73]

The Magisterium of the Church

85 "The task of giving an authentic interpretation of the Word of God, whether in its written form or in the form of Tradition, has been entrusted to the living teaching office of the Church alone. Its authority in this matter is exercised in the name of Jesus Christ."[74] This means that the task of interpretation has been entrusted to the bishops in communion with the successor of Peter, the Bishop of Rome.

86 "Yet this Magisterium is not superior to the Word of God, but is its servant. It teaches only what has been handed on to it. At the divine command and with the help of the Holy Spirit, it listens to this devotedly, guards it with dedication, and expounds it faithfully. All that it proposes for belief as being divinely revealed is drawn from this single deposit of faith."[75]

87 Mindful of Christ's words to his apostles: "He who hears you, hears me",[76] the faithful receive with docility the teachings and directives that their pastors give them in different forms.

The dogmas of the faith

88 The Church's Magisterium exercises the authority it holds from Christ to the fullest extent when it defines dogmas, that is, when it proposes, in a form obliging the Christian

---

73 *DV* 10 § 1; cf. *Acts* 2:42 (Gk.); Pius XII, apostolic constitution, *Munificentissimus Deus*, November 1, 1950: AAS 42 (1950), 756, taken along with the words of St. Cyprian, Epist. 66, 8: CSEL 3, 2, 733: "The Church is the people united to its Priests, the flock adhering to its Shepherd."

74 *DV* 10 § 2.

75 *DV* 10 § 2.

76 *Lk* 10:16; cf. LG 20.

people to an irrevocable adherence of faith, truths contained in divine Revelation or also when it proposes, in a definitive way, truths having a necessary connection with these.

89 There is an organic connection between our spiritual life and the dogmas. Dogmas are lights along the path of faith; they illuminate it and make it secure. Conversely, if our life is upright, our intellect and heart will be open to welcome the light shed by the dogmas of faith.[77]

90 The mutual connections between dogmas, and their coherence, can be found in the whole of the Revelation of the mystery of Christ.[78] "In Catholic doctrine there exists an order or hierarchy of truths, since they vary in their relation to the foundation of the Christian faith."[79]

The supernatural sense of faith

91 All the faithful share in understanding and handing on revealed truth. They have received the anointing of the Holy Spirit, who instructs them[80] and guides them into all truth.[81]

92 "The whole body of the faithful... cannot err in matters of belief. This characteristic is shown in the supernatural appreciation of faith (*sensus fidei*) on the part of the whole people, when, from the bishops to the last of the faithful, they manifest a universal consent in matters of faith and morals."[82]

93 "By this appreciation of the faith, aroused and sustained by the Spirit of truth, the People of God, guided by the sacred teaching authority (*Magisterium*), ... receives ... the faith,

77 Cf. *Jn* 8:31–32.

78 Cf. Vatican Council I:DS 3016: *nexus mysteriorum*; LG 25.

79 *UR* 11.

80 Cf. 1 *Jn* 2:20, 27.

81 Cf. *Jn* 16:13.

82 *LG* 12; cf. St. Augustine, *De praed. sanct.* 14, 27: PL 44, 980.

once for all delivered to the saints ... The People unfailingly adheres to this faith, penetrates it more deeply with right judgment, and applies it more fully in daily life."[83]

Growth in understanding the faith

94 Thanks to the assistance of the Holy Spirit, the understanding of both the realities and the words of the heritage of faith is able to grow in the life of the Church:

— "through the contemplation and study of believers who ponder these things in their hearts";[84] it is in particular "theological research [which] deepens knowledge of revealed truth".[85]

— "from the intimate sense of spiritual realities which [believers] experience",[86] the sacred Scriptures "grow with the one who reads them."[87]

— "from the preaching of those who have received, along with their right of succession in the episcopate, the sure charism of truth."[88]

95 "It is clear therefore that, in the supremely wise arrangement of God, sacred Tradition, Sacred Scripture, and the Magisterium of the Church are so connected and associated that one of them cannot stand without the others. Working together, each in its own way, under the action of the one Holy Spirit, they all contribute effectively to the salvation of souls."[89]

---

83 *LG* 12; cf. *Jude* 3.

84 *DV* 8 § 2; cf. *Lk* 2:19, 51.

85 *GS* 62 § 7; cf. *GS* 44 § 2; *DV* 23; 24; *UR* 4.

86 *DV* 8 § 2.

87 St. Gregory the Great, Hom. in *Ez.* 1, 7, 8: PL 76, 843D.

88 *DV* 8 § 2.

89 *DV* 10 § 3.

IN BRIEF

96 What Christ entrusted to the apostles, they in turn handed on by their preaching and writing, under the inspiration of the Holy Spirit, to all generations, until Christ returns in glory.

97 "Sacred Tradition and Sacred Scripture make up a single sacred deposit of the Word of God" (*DV* 10), in which, as in a mirror, the pilgrim Church contemplates God, the source of all her riches.

98 "The Church, in her doctrine, life, and worship, perpetuates and transmits to every generation all that she herself is, all that she believes" (*DV* 8 §1).

99 Thanks to its supernatural sense of faith, the People of God as a whole never ceases to welcome, to penetrate more deeply, and to live more fully from the gift of divine Revelation.

100 The task of interpreting the Word of God authentically has been entrusted solely to the Magisterium of the Church, that is, to the Pope and to the bishops in communion with him.

ARTICLE 3: SACRED SCRIPTURE

I. CHRIST — THE UNIQUE WORD OF SACRED SCRIPTURE

101 In order to reveal himself to men, in the condescension of his goodness God speaks to them in human words: "Indeed the words of God, expressed in the words of men, are in every way like human language, just as the Word of the eternal Father, when he took on himself the flesh of human weakness, became like men."[90]

----

90 *DV* 13.

102 Through all the words of Sacred Scripture, God speaks only one single Word, his one Utterance in whom he expresses himself completely:[91]

> You recall that one and the same Word of God extends throughout Scripture, that it is one and the same Utterance that resounds in the mouths of all the sacred writers, since he who was in the beginning God with God has no need of separate syllables; for he is not subject to time.[92]

103 For this reason, the Church has always venerated the Scriptures as she venerates the Lord's Body. She never ceases to present to the faithful the bread of life, taken from the one table of God's Word and Christ's Body.[93]

104 In Sacred Scripture, the Church constantly finds her nourishment and her strength, for she welcomes it not as a human word, "but as what it really is, the word of God".[94] "In the sacred books, the Father who is in heaven comes lovingly to meet his children, and talks with them."[95]

II. INSPIRATION AND TRUTH OF SACRED SCRIPTURE

105 *God is the author of Sacred Scripture.* "The divinely revealed realities, which are contained and presented in the text of Sacred Scripture, have been written down under the inspiration of the Holy Spirit."[96]

"For Holy Mother Church, relying on the faith of the apostolic age, accepts as sacred and canonical the books of the Old and the New Testaments, whole and entire, with all

---

91 Cf. *Heb* 1:1–3.

92 St. Augustine, *En. in Ps.* 103, 4, 1: PL 37, 1378; cf. *Ps* 104; *Jn* 1:1.

93 Cf. *DV* 21.

94 *1 Thess* 2:13; cf. *DV* 24.

95 *DV* 21.

96 *DV* 11.

their parts, on the grounds that, written under the inspiration of the Holy Spirit, they have God as their author and have been handed on as such to the Church herself."[97]

106 God inspired the human authors of the sacred books. "To compose the sacred books, God chose certain men who, all the while he employed them in this task, made full use of their own faculties and powers so that, though he acted in them and by them, it was as true authors that they consigned to writing whatever he wanted written, and no more."[98]

107 The inspired books teach the truth. "Since therefore all that the inspired authors or sacred writers affirm should be regarded as affirmed by the Holy Spirit, we must acknowledge that the books of Scripture firmly, faithfully, and without error teach that truth which God, for the sake of our salvation, wished to see confided to the Sacred Scriptures."[99]

108 Still, the Christian faith is not a "religion of the book." Christianity is the religion of the "Word" of God, a word which is "not a written and mute word, but the Word which is incarnate and living."[100] If the Scriptures are not to remain a dead letter, Christ, the eternal Word of the living God, must, through the Holy Spirit, "open [our] minds to understand the Scriptures."[101]

III. THE HOLY SPIRIT, INTERPRETER OF SCRIPTURE

109 In Sacred Scripture, God speaks to man in a human way. To interpret Scripture correctly, the reader must be attentive to what the human authors truly wanted to affirm and to what God wanted to reveal to us by their words.[102]

....

97 *DV* 11; cf. *Jn* 20:31; *2 Tim* 3:16; *2 Pet* 1:19–21; 3:15–16.

98 *DV* 11.

99 *DV* 11.

100 St. Bernard, *S. missus est hom.* 4, 11: PL 183, 86.

101 Cf. *Lk* 24:45.

102 Cf. *DV* 12 § 1.

110 In order to discover *the sacred authors' intention*, the reader must take into account the conditions of their time and culture, the literary genres in use at that time, and the modes of feeling, speaking, and narrating then current. "For the fact is that truth is differently presented and expressed in the various types of historical writing, in prophetical and poetical texts, and in other forms of literary expression."[103]

111 But since Sacred Scripture is inspired, there is another and no less important principle of correct interpretation, without which Scripture would remain a dead letter. "Sacred Scripture must be read and interpreted in the light of the same Spirit by whom it was written."[104]

The Second Vatican Council indicates three criteria for interpreting Scripture in accordance with the Spirit who inspired it.[105]

112 1. *Be especially attentive "to the content and unity of the whole Scripture."* Different as the books which comprise it may be, Scripture is a unity by reason of the unity of God's plan, of which Christ Jesus is the center and heart, open since his Passover.[106]

> The phrase "heart of Christ" can refer to Sacred Scripture, which makes known his heart, closed before the Passion, as the Scripture was obscure. But the Scripture has been opened since the Passion; since those who from then on have understood it, consider and discern in what way the prophecies must be interpreted.[107]

---

103 *DV* 12 § 2.

104 *DV* 12 § 3.

105 Cf. *DV* 12 § 4.

106 Cf. *Lk* 24:25–27, 44–46.

107 St. Thomas Aquinas, *Expos. in Ps* 21,11; cf. *Ps* 22:15.

113 2. *Read the Scripture within "the living Tradition of the whole Church."* According to a saying of the Fathers, Sacred Scripture is written principally in the Church's heart rather than in documents and records, for the Church carries in her Tradition the living memorial of God's Word, and it is the Holy Spirit who gives her the spiritual interpretation of the Scripture ("according to the spiritual meaning which the Spirit grants to the Church"[108]).

114 3. *Be attentive to the analogy of faith.*[109] By "analogy of faith" we mean the coherence of the truths of faith among themselves and within the whole plan of Revelation.

The senses of Scripture

115 According to an ancient tradition, one can distinguish between two *senses* of Scripture: the literal and the spiritual, the latter being subdivided into the allegorical, moral, and anagogical senses. The profound concordance of the four senses guarantees all its richness to the living reading of Scripture in the Church.

116 The *literal sense* is the meaning conveyed by the words of Scripture and discovered by exegesis, following the rules of sound interpretation: "All other senses of Sacred Scripture are based on the literal."[110]

117 The *spiritual sense.* Thanks to the unity of God's plan, not only the text of Scripture but also the realities and events about which it speaks can be signs.

1. The *allegorical sense.* We can acquire a more profound understanding of events by recognizing their significance in Christ; thus the crossing of the Red Sea is a sign or type of Christ's victory and also of Christian Baptism.[111]

---

108 Origen, *Hom. in Lev.* 5, 5: PG 12, 454D.
109 Cf. *Rom* 12:6.
110 St. Thomas Aquinas, *STh* I, 1, 10, ad 1.
111 Cf. *1 Cor* 10:2.

2. The *moral sense*. The events reported in Scripture ought to lead us to act justly. As St. Paul says, they were written "for our instruction."[112]

3. The *anagogical sense* (Greek: *anagoge*, "leading"). We can view realities and events in terms of their eternal significance, leading us toward our true homeland: thus the Church on earth is a sign of the heavenly Jerusalem.[113]

118 A medieval couplet summarizes the significance of the four senses:

> The Letter speaks of deeds; Allegory to faith;
> The Moral how to act; Anagogy our destiny.[114]

119 "It is the task of exegetes to work, according to these rules, towards a better understanding and explanation of the meaning of Sacred Scripture in order that their research may help the Church to form a firmer judgment. For, of course, all that has been said about the manner of interpreting Scripture is ultimately subject to the judgment of the Church which exercises the divinely conferred commission and ministry of watching over and interpreting the Word of God."[115]

> But I would not believe in the Gospel, had not the authority of the Catholic Church already moved me.[116]

IV. THE CANON OF SCRIPTURE

120 It was by the apostolic Tradition that the Church discerned which writings are to be included in the list of the sacred

112 *1 Cor* 10:11; cf. *Heb* 3:1–4:11.

113 Cf. *Rev* 21:1–22:5.

114 Littera gesta docet, quid credas allegoria, moralis quid agas, quo tendas anagogia; Augustine of Dacia, *Rotulus pugillaris*, I: ed. A. Walz: Angelicum 6 (1929) 256.

115 *DV* 12 § 3.

116 St. Augustine, *Contra epistolam Manichaei*, 5, 6: PL 42, 176.

books.[117] This complete list is called the canon of Scripture. It includes 46 books for the Old Testament (45 if we count Jeremiah and Lamentations as one) and 27 for the New.[118]

The Old Testament: Genesis, Exodus, Leviticus, Numbers, Deuteronomy, Joshua, Judges, Ruth, 1 *and* 2 Samuel, 1 *and* 2 Kings, 1 *and* 2 Chronicles, Ezra *and* Nehemiah, Tobit, Judith, Esther, 1 *and* 2 Maccabees, Job, Psalms, Proverbs, Ecclesiastes, *the* Song of Songs, *the* Wisdom of Solomon, Sirach (Ecclesiasticus), Isaiah, Jeremiah, Lamentations, Baruch, Ezekiel, Daniel, Hosea, Joel, Amos, Obadiah, Jonah, Micah, Nahum, Habakkuk, Zephaniah, Haggai, Zechariah *and* Malachi.

The New Testament: *the* Gospels according to Matthew, Mark, Luke *and* John, *the* Acts of *the* Apostles, *the* Letters of St. Paul to *the* Romans, 1 *and* 2 Corinthians, Galatians, Ephesians, Philippians, Colossians, 1 *and* 2 Thessalonians, 1 *and* 2 Timothy, Titus, Philemon, *the* Letter to *the* Hebrews, *the* Letters of James, 1 *and* 2 Peter, 1, 2, *and* 3 John, *and* Jude, *and* Revelation (the Apocalypse).

The Old Testament

121 The Old Testament is an indispensable part of Sacred Scripture. Its books are divinely inspired and retain a permanent value,[119] for the Old Covenant has never been revoked.

122 Indeed, "the economy of the Old Testament was deliberately so oriented that it should prepare for and declare in prophecy the coming of Christ, redeemer of all men."[120] "Even though they contain matters imperfect and provisional,"[121] the books of the Old Testament bear witness to the whole

---

117 Cf. *DV* 8 § 3.
118 Cf. DS 179; 1334–1336; 1501–1504.
119 Cf. *DV* 14.
120 *DV* 15.
121 *DV* 15.

divine pedagogy of God's saving love: these writings "are a storehouse of sublime teaching on God and of sound wisdom on human life, as well as a wonderful treasury of prayers; in them, too, the mystery of our salvation is present in a hidden way."[122]

123 Christians venerate the Old Testament as true Word of God. The Church has always vigorously opposed the idea of rejecting the Old Testament under the pretext that the New has rendered it void (Marcionism).

The New Testament

124 "The Word of God, which is the power of God for salvation to everyone who has faith, is set forth and displays its power in a most wonderful way in the writings of the New Testament"[123] which hand on the ultimate truth of God's Revelation. Their central object is Jesus Christ, God's incarnate Son: his acts, teachings, Passion and glorification, and his Church's beginnings under the Spirit's guidance.[124]

125 The *Gospels* are the heart of all the Scriptures "because they are our principal source for the life and teaching of the Incarnate Word, our Savior".[125]

126 We can distinguish three stages in the formation of the Gospels:

1. *The life and teaching of Jesus.* The Church holds firmly that the four Gospels, "whose historicity she unhesitatingly affirms, faithfully hand on what Jesus, the Son of God, while he lived among men, really did and taught for their eternal salvation, until the day when he was taken up."[126]

---

122 *DV* 15.
123 *DV* 17; cf. *Rom* 1:16.
124 Cf. *DV* 20.
125 *DV* 18.
126 *DV* 19; cf. *Acts* 1:1--2.

2. *The oral tradition.* "For, after the ascension of the Lord, the apostles handed on to their hearers what he had said and done, but with that fuller understanding which they, instructed by the glorious events of Christ and enlightened by the Spirit of truth, now enjoyed."[127]

3. *The written Gospels.* "The sacred authors, in writing the four Gospels, selected certain of the many elements which had been handed on, either orally or already in written form; others they synthesized or explained with an eye to the situation of the churches, while sustaining the form of preaching, but always in such a fashion that they have told us the honest truth about Jesus."[128]

127 The fourfold Gospel holds a unique place in the Church, as is evident both in the veneration which the liturgy accords it and in the surpassing attraction it has exercised on the saints at all times:

> There is no doctrine which could be better, more precious and more splendid than the text of the Gospel. Behold and retain what our Lord and Master, Christ, has taught by his words and accomplished by his deeds.[129]

> But above all it's the gospels that occupy my mind when I'm at prayer; my poor soul has so many needs, and yet this is the one thing needful. I'm always finding fresh lights there; hidden and enthralling meanings.[130]

127 *DV* 19.
128 *DV* 19.
129 St. Caesaria the Younger to St. Richildis and St. Radegunde, SCh 345, 480.
130 St. Thérèse of Lisieux, *ms. autob.* A 83v.

The unity of the Old and New Testaments

128 The Church, as early as apostolic times,[131] and then constantly in her Tradition, has illuminated the unity of the divine plan in the two Testaments through typology, which discerns in God's works of the Old Covenant prefigurations of what he accomplished in the fullness of time in the person of his incarnate Son.

129 Christians therefore read the Old Testament in the light of Christ crucified and risen. Such typological reading discloses the inexhaustible content of the Old Testament; but it must not make us forget that the Old Testament retains its own intrinsic value as Revelation reaffirmed by our Lord himself.[132] Besides, the New Testament has to be read in the light of the Old. Early Christian catechesis made constant use of the Old Testament.[133] As an old saying put it, the New Testament lies hidden in the Old and the Old Testament is unveiled in the New.[134]

130 Typology indicates the dynamic movement toward the fulfillment of the divine plan when "God [will] be everything to everyone."[135] Nor do the calling of the patriarchs and the exodus from Egypt, for example, lose their own value in God's plan, from the mere fact that they were intermediate stages.

V. SACRED SCRIPTURE IN THE LIFE OF THE CHURCH

131 "And such is the force and power of the Word of God that it can serve the Church as her support and vigor and the children of the Church as strength for their faith, food for

---

131 Cf. *1 Cor* 10:6, 11; *Heb* 10:1; *l Pet* 3:21.

132 Cf. *Mk* 12:29–31.

133 Cf. *1 Cor* 5:6–8; 10:1–11.

134 Cf. St. Augustine, *Quaest. in Hept.* 2, 73: PL 34, 623; cf. *DV* 16.

135 *1 Cor* 15:28.

the soul, and a pure and lasting fount of spiritual life."[136] Hence "access to Sacred Scripture ought to be open wide to the Christian faithful."[137]

132 "Therefore, the 'study of the sacred page' should be the very soul of sacred theology. The ministry of the Word, too — pastoral preaching, catechetics, and all forms of Christian instruction, among which the liturgical homily should hold pride of place — is healthily nourished and thrives in holiness through the Word of Scripture."[138]

133 The Church "forcefully and specifically exhorts all the Christian faithful ... to learn 'the surpassing knowledge of Jesus Christ,' by frequent reading of the divine Scriptures. 'Ignorance of the Scriptures is ignorance of Christ.'"[139]

IN BRIEF

134 All Sacred Scripture is but one book, and this one book is Christ, "because all divine Scripture speaks of Christ, and all divine Scripture is fulfilled in Christ" (Hugh of St. Victor, *De arca Noe* 2, 8: PL 176, 642: cf. ibid. 2, 9: PL 176, 642–643).

135 "The Sacred Scriptures contain the Word of God and, because they are inspired, they are truly the Word of God" (*DV* 24).

136 God is the author of Sacred Scripture because he inspired its human authors; he acts in them and by means of them. He thus gives assurance that their writings teach without error his saving truth (cf. *DV* 11).

137 Interpretation of the inspired Scripture must be attentive above all to what God wants to reveal through the sacred authors for our salvation. What comes from the Spirit is

136 *DV* 21.

137 *DV* 22.

138 *DV* 24.

139 *DV* 25; cf. Phil 3:8 and St. Jerome, *Commentariorum in Isaiam libri xviii* prol.: PL 24, 17b.

not fully "understood except by the Spirit's action" (cf. Origen, *Hom. in Ex.* 4, 5: PG 12, 320).

138 The Church accepts and venerates as inspired the 46 books of the Old Testament and the 27 books of the New.

139 The four Gospels occupy a central place because Christ Jesus is their center.

140 The unity of the two Testaments proceeds from the unity of God's plan and his Revelation. The Old Testament prepares for the New and the New Testament fulfills the Old; the two shed light on each other; both are true Word of God.

141 "The Church has always venerated the divine Scriptures as she venerated the Body of the Lord" (*DV* 21): both nourish and govern the whole Christian life. "Your word is a lamp to my feet and a light to my path" (*Ps* 119:105; cf. *Isa* 50:4).

EPILOGUE:
SOLA SCRIPTURA: A STONY PATH

Before you object to what has been said in the preceding chapters, please consider carefully the implications of the following passage from Deuteronomy (12:32–13:5):

> Everything that I command you, you shall be careful to do; you shall not add to it or take from it.
>
> If a prophet arises among you, or a dreamer of dreams, and gives you a sign or a wonder, and the sign or wonder which he tells you comes to pass, and if he says, "Let us go after other gods," which you have not known, "and let us serve them," you shall not listen to the words of that prophet or to that dreamer of dreams; for the Lord your God is testing you, to know whether you love the Lord your God with all your heart and with all your soul. You shall walk after the Lord your God and fear him, and keep his commandments and obey his voice, and you shall serve him and cling to him. But that prophet or that dreamer of dreams shall be put to death, because he has taught rebellion against the Lord your God, who brought you out of the land of Egypt and redeemed you out of the house of bondage, to make you leave the way in which the Lord your God commanded you to walk. So you shall purge the evil from the midst of you.

As you consider the above passage, remember that when Jesus confounded the devil during His forty days in the desert, He relied upon the authority and truth of this book (Deut 8:3; 6:16; and 6:13). When he summarized the Law into the

Greatest Commandment, He again confirmed the authority of this and other books of Moses (Deut 6:5 and Lev 19:18). Also, remember that it is upon the fact that Jesus quoted from these books that most Protestant scholars, preachers, and teachers begin building the doctrine of *sola Scriptura*.

Now considering this passage, how would you, or should you, interpret and apply this passage if you were the pastor of an independent Christian Bible church, responsible to no one but Jesus through the Holy Spirit? What are you to do with those prophets and dreamers in your midst who claim private messages from God and who then attempt to pull people from your congregation in directions different from where you believe God is calling you? Let's say you have chosen to teach your people the Trinitarian formulas of the third– and fourth–century ecumenical councils, while these new leaders — confirmed by signs and wonders — are teaching that the so-called doctrine of the Trinity is just papist tradition and that God is found only in Jesus or in the Holy Spirit. What should you do with these teachers of rebellion?

Now I suppose having them stoned seems a bit violent in our modern, civilized (?) society, but this was the prescribed punishment of choice, described in Scripture: "You shall stone him to death with stones, because he sought to draw you away from the Lord your God ... And all Israel shall hear, and fear, and never again do any such wickedness as this among you" (Deut 13:10–11).

You can tell by the wording of this passage that there were still a few of the leaders flinging sheep[140] for this punishment, but more importantly you can see that there is great benefit to the future stability of your congregation if you heed these instructions from God's Word.

---

140 Why else would Moses need to be redundant about emphasizing that stoning is to be done with stones?

Now you might say that as the New Testament Church you are not bound by these Old Testament Jewish regulations. However, as emphatically as the Apostle Paul may have exhorted his followers to cease being slaves to the Law, when push came to shove, he confessed his unswerving loyalty to it: "But this I admit to you, that according to the Way, which they call a sect, I worship the God of our fathers, *believing everything laid down by the law or written in the prophets*" (Acts 24:14, emphasis added).

What will you tell your elders and congregation they should do with the schismatics in your midst? And what about those of your congregation who follow them, for the Scriptures command that you stone them as well (Deut 13:6–11)? How will you handle any fights that may break out amongst your warring flock? The Scriptures are very strict about what must be done (you must read Deut 25:11–12!).

Now I'm not bringing these regulations to your attention because I think we should rethink how we deal with schismatics or family squabbles. Rather, I'm pointing out how dangerous the doctrine of *sola Scriptura* can be and has been ever since it was first coined by the sixteenth–century Reformers. When the wisdom and guidance of Sacred Tradition and the Church Magisterium were thrown to the wind, Christendom fell victim to "every wind of doctrine" (Eph 4:14). In fact, it was in this context that Paul begged the Ephesian believers to "maintain the unity of the Spirit," recognizing that Christ had gifted His Body with Apostles, prophets, evangelists, pastors, and teachers to enable the Church to "attain to the unity of the Faith" (Eph 4:1–16).

Now granted, some of the men and women who have held these positions of church leadership throughout her history have done much to sever this unity. Some have made unity so downright uncomfortable that one could nearly justify breaking free to be all that Paul exhorted a Church to be. But then on what side of Deuteronomy 13 would one fall? And once you've successfully dodged all the stones, when might you need to start throwing stones of your own?

Recently, I become more sensitized to these dangers of *sola Scriptura.* Following the Coming Home Network's *Read the Bible and Catechism in a Year* brochure, I was attempting to read the Bible straight through from cover to cover for the first time since I graduated from seminary over thirty years ago. In doing so, my eyes were becoming newly opened to the vast number of Scripture passages that can pose grave difficulties for modern interpreters. As I ruminate on my years as a Protestant pastor, I'm now much more aware of how I unconsciously categorized Bible passages into those that I assumed were easily interpreted and preached (such as Jn 3:16, Rom 8:28, or Gal 2:20) from those that needed quick explanations (such as those previously referenced above, as well as Mt 16:16–19, Jn 6:51ff, Heb 6:4–6, and Jas 2:24). I have come to realize that we Protestant clergy had an unspoken way of dealing with difficult, uncomfortable verses like the latter list. We'd essentially let them sit until we heard or read someone we highly respected give a plausible, believable, repeatable answer — that also passed the litmus tests of our other accepted dogma. This we then memorized and added to our list of quick knee-jerk responses. The grave difficulty with this is that, from then on, we assumed that these verses were no longer difficult or uncomfortable — and we would communicate this to our congregations. Over time, we had quick answers for all hard verses, which allowed us to essentially ignore any challenges they might pose to our theologies or morals. And these quick answers enabled us to ignore the contradictory ways that other faithful Christians interpreted these difficult and uncomfortable passages. So to what extent were we following Scripture *alone* or merely reshaping Scripture to no longer be hard or uncomfortable?

I strongly encourage all of you, Catholic or Protestant, to give God's word this attention: read carefully through the entire Bible, even those passages that are a bit tedious. As you do so, be sure to note the many, many verses that are not so easy to explain at first glance. When you do — if you do — I strongly encourage you to recognize with great thanksgiving how gracious and loving Christ our Savior was when He gave us the Church guided by His Spirit. Obedience to Her might keep us all from becoming rightful candidates for stoning!

AFTERWORD

It is appropriate to explain that this book has a history, since I owe most of its content to a committee of authors. Originally, the content of this book was in the form of a journal on the topic of *sola Scriptura* published in 1997. It consisted of a collection of loosely related articles, by separate authors, all centered on the topic of *sola Scriptura*. Over the years, the journal has gone through several edits and reprintings, until recently, the cupboard of its remaining issues had become bare.

Given the revision of the very mission of our apostolate — to focus more proactively on sharing through media the beauty and truth of the Catholic Christian Faith with non-Catholic Christians — we saw the need to either revise the journal or scrap it entirely to make room for another, more unified book on the subject. What we decided to do was a combination of both: use the previous collection of articles as the foundation for a thoroughly revised, rearranged, even rewritten, unified volume, with the goal of producing one flowing examination of the Protestant doctrine of *sola Scriptura*. To the extent that the finished product approaches this goal is completely traceable to the original authors, whose convictions and writings provided the meat, while I did little more than blend them together, if you will, into the casserole. I pray this work is an encouragement to you, the reader, and that it helps you draw closer to Jesus Christ and His Church.

In Christ,
Marcus Grodi

HOW TO BECOME A MEMBER OF *THE COMING HOME NETWORK INTERNATIONAL* AND SUPPORT ITS WORK

The Coming Home Network International was established to help inquiring non-Catholic clergy as well as laity come home and then be at home in the Catholic Church. Through the one-on-one outreach of our pastoral staff, our monthly CHNewsletter, regional retreats, and our online community forums and groups at CHNetwork.org, we strive to ensure that each person touched by grace has the fellowship and resources they need to discover the truth and beauty of the Catholic Faith.

WE PROVIDE

■ **Contacts, assistance, and fellowship** for those who are exploring the teaching and history of the Catholic Church, and are considering coming into full communion with the Church;

■ **Continued fellowship and encouragement** for those who have entered the Church and want to live fully Catholic lives;

■ **Conversion stories** to provide inspiration for those on the journey and those already Catholic. We have one of the largest online collections of conversion stories on our website www.chnetwork.org, including nearly 20 years worth of episodes of the *The Journey Home* program, along with numerous written stories, podcasts, and other articles related to the Catholic Faith.

■ **Books and other resources** that give clear expressions of the Catholic Faith.

HOW CAN I BECOME A MEMBER?

If you are interested in becoming a member of the CHNetwork, please contact us:

Website: chnetwork.org
E-mail: info@chnetwork.org
Phone: 740-450-1175
Mail: Coming Home Network International
PO Box 8290 Zanesville, OH 43702-8290